THE Bully Solution

A PARENT'S GUIDE

D1373170

Carol McMullen

■SCHOLASTIC

NEW YORK • TORONTO • LONDON • AUCKLAND • SYDNEY
MEXICO CITY • NEW DELHI • HONG KONG • BUENOS AIRES

This book is dedicated to my Mom and Dad, who have always believed in me (even when I didn't) and to my husband John, whose love, support, and encouragement makes my life complete.

Edited by Sarah Longhi

Content editing by Rebecca Callan

Cover design by Brian LaRossa

Interior design by Melinda Belter

Interior photo credits: page 6 © Superstudio/Gettyimages, page 11 © Caroline Woodham/Gettyimages, page 25 © Randy Faris/Jupiter Images, page 47 © Maria Sweeney/Gettyimages, page 48 © Polka Dot Images/Jupiter Images, page 74 © Darrin Klimek/Gettyimages, page 93 © Jupiter Images, page 107 © Joseph Sohm/Jupiter Images, page 124 © Bruce Laurence/Gettyimages

Comic strip page 130 © 2007 by Daniel Shelton. Reprinted by permission of the author.

ISBN-13 978-0-439-02422-8

ISBN-10 0-439-02422-6

Contents

Bullies have been a part of life since time immemorial. Everyone has been bullied, and if we're honest with ourselves, most of us have bullied others at some point in our lives.

~*Carol McMullen*

Introduction

Bullying is a behavior that takes various forms and affects most children in one way or another. Our society is constantly inundated with examples of bullying behavior. News broadcasts, television programs, music videos, and movies all provide myriad examples of how to bully and few examples of appropriate ways to handle bullying situations. Because violent, aggressive behavior surrounds us, we should not be particularly surprised when we see these same behaviors in familiar settings—the park, bus stop, and so on.

It's important to catch bullying behaviors at an early stage in your child's development. With proper monitoring and support, it is possible to redirect young children and prevent them from getting the attention and feelings of power that come with bullying—payoffs that reinforce it. At the same time, we can help bullied children recognize their strengths and develop strategies to deal with problematic situations more successfully. Helping children learn appropriate interpersonal skills affords us an opportunity to make a difference before behaviors harden into self-defeating and possibly dangerous patterns.

Over the past few years, more attention has been focused on bullying as parents and educators begin to fully realize the negative impact it has upon children. Is this because bullying incidents are becoming more violent? Possibly. What people are beginning to acknowledge is that bullying is a form of violence and the time has come to deal with the issue directly.

About This Book

As you have likely discovered, theory is useful, but you and your child need specific, nuts-and-bolts, structured information about bullying and how to handle bullying situations. Over more than 20 years of teaching, I developed a practical guide of methods, tips, and techniques that work to the benefit of both bullied children and bullies. This book, the result, focuses on key areas of child growth and development: self-esteem, assertiveness

In Action: Ben and Chad

A note was in my mailbox when I arrived that Monday morning. I glanced at it and sighed. It was from one of my parents, Mrs. Lewis, asking me to call about an incident involving her son Ben and another of my students, Chad. I already suspected what the call was about. Chad had been harassing Ben since the beginning of the school year and, in spite of my warnings, things had apparently not improved.

I was right. Chad had sworn at Ben and pushed him down at recess before taking his recess snack. "I didn't know anything about it," I said, frustrated.

"I think Ben feels that there's no point in telling you," Mrs. Lewis replied. "He tried to get help from you before, but he says Chad is still bullying him. He feels pretty hopeless about all this, and he's starting to kick up a fuss about coming to school. I don't know what to do. I may try and contact Chad's parents but I think we need help. What should I do?"

During my years as a classroom teacher, I had conversations like this with many parents who were just as overwhelmed and frustrated as their children were. Ben's situation became my catalyst because I realized that I, too, had few ideas about how to help children deal with bullies. So I developed a comprehensive program to teach bully-proofing skills to my classes, as I described in my first book, *Creating a Bully-Free Classroom*. I quickly realized that these same ideas could certainly be taught and used at home, and this book was born.

We were able to resolve Ben's situation that year, and one of the keys to this process was helping Ben develop his self-confidence and coping strategies. There are many techniques that do just that and are easily taught and practiced at home and at school.

(and not aggressiveness), empathy, friendship, and conflict resolution.

The ideas and activities in this book are supported by research and practice. The activities and strategies I've developed are based upon the essential premise that all children—bullies and bullied alike—benefit from specific lessons that emphasize problem-solving strategies, recognizing and using personal strengths, and developing skills for relating successfully to others.

The problem of bullying has many layers. There is no one magical, quick solution. Rather, the issue must be approached from many angles. To that end, in *The Bully Solution: A Parent's Guide*, I've grouped bully-proofing activities and strategies into seven chapters. Each of the chapters provides guidance for creating successful bully-proofing plans, one for you to use as a parent and one to meet the specific needs of your child.

The objective of Chapter One, **A Bullying Primer**, is to provide an overview of bullying issues. It begins with facts and research about bullying and moves to topics including characteristics of bullies, bullied children, and bystanders. These topics are accompanied by challenging questions intended to make you question your assumptions. Next, the chapter explores important differences between conflict and bullying, the dual responsibilities of parents as adult role models and as caregivers, and the steps you can take to help your child.

The focus of Chapter Two, **What Can I Do to Help?**, is assisting children who are vulnerable to bullying. In this chapter, you will find invitations to think about the discipline philosophy you follow to guide your child, and about what works and what doesn't. You will also find opportunities to think about what you and your child could do in the future and ways of distilling those ideas into personalized plans of action. You will learn why it is essential for you and your child to be proactive, and have a sense of control and confidence that will help you deal with a bully if you need to. Finally, you'll learn about practical ways to ensure that you, your child, and your child's school are working collaboratively . . . and with your child in mind.

Chapter Three moves from the theoretical to the practical. In **Bully-Proofing** you will be introduced to many techniques and practical ideas for dealing with bullies. Some topics included are talking with your child about bullying in general, using literature to support your discussions, and working with your child to develop a bully-proofing plan. As you move through the chapter, you'll find that the strategies and activities presented are geared toward developing self-esteem—encouraging your child to say to himself or herself, "I can do this. I can handle this." This chapter also includes a compilation of the Top Ten Strategies for Handling Bullies.

Chapter Four, **What If the Bully Is My Child?**, looks at the issue from the other side. Sometimes a parent of a child who exhibits patterns of bullying behaviors may need to seek outside intervention. Most times though, there are things you as a parent can do. You can help support your child's growth and development of constructive behaviors, including exploring empathy and expressing anger appropriately. And in this chapter, you will find suggestions for helping your child experience positive interactions with other people and accept responsibility for aggressive behavior.

As adults, we tend to assume that children naturally know how to be friends with others. But the reality is that many children need specific guidance about how to make and be a friend. The strategies and activities in Chapter Five, **We All Need Friends**, focus on factors for building successful relationships. Where there is broad discussion about certain social skills, you'll also find detailed descriptions of honing listening skills and decoding body language. This chapter closes with information about empathy and the ways in which it can serve us in our exchanges with others.

Chapter Six, **Conflict Resolution**, presents a structured four-step resolution model that helps children resolve conflicts. Using this model, children practice solving problems with their peers or siblings. They become skilled at identifying the main issue, discussing it, and working together to come up with a resolution. In this chapter you'll learn how to become a coach. You will also learn how conflict resolution works and why it enables your child to talk out problems comfortably and confidently and take ownership of the problem-solving process.

In Chapter Seven, **Cyber Bullying**, you'll discover practical ways of preventing cyber bullying and tactics for dealing with it. And to help you face the challenges cyber bullying presents, I've included suggestions about how you can help your child navigate the Internet safely. Plus, you'll find useful techniques for spotting cyber bullying in action and tips for deciphering those abbreviations and acronyms that children use with ease (and with which they keep parents in the dark).

In the appendices of *The Bully Solution*, I've included a collection of pages that support the activities and strategies presented. You'll find fill-in templates you can photocopy and use right away, lists of resources and references to help keep you well informed, and an index you can use to pinpoint the information you need.

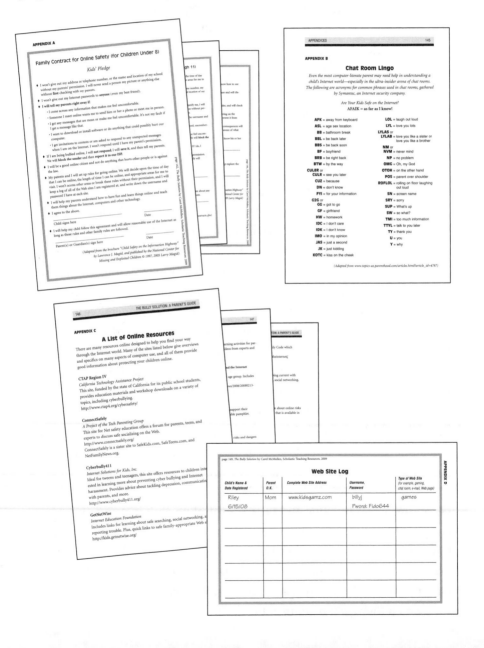

I have great faith in "ordinary parents." Who has a child's welfare more at heart than his ordinary parent? It's been my experience that when parents are given the skills to be more helpful, not only are they able to use these skills, but they infuse them with a warmth and a style that is uniquely their own.

~Haim Ginott,
child psychologist

CHAPTER ONE

A Bullying Primer

As a classroom teacher I often spoke with parents desperate for ways to help their children deal with bullies. I found it difficult because I didn't have many answers myself. What I came to know over time is that as parents, you have the power to create environments that promote tolerance, acceptance, and justice. You and your child will have the power to actively deny bullies their power.

Families, school administrators, researchers, and many other concerned people are in search of solutions to this exasperating, often insidious behavior. What I had been doing wasn't particularly effective at helping prevent bullying. The more I realized that I needed new ways of dealing effectively with bullying, the more I realized I needed to research the best way of supporting my students. As I gained knowledge on the subject of bullying, I decided to focus my efforts on researching bully-proofing strategies and techniques.

Andy came home from school on Thursday upset, and his shirt pocket was torn off. After a lot of prodding, he told me that Ste had been picking on him again Steve's been taunting him at school and then tracking him down on the walk home. I don't feel right telling And to fight back, which is who his father says he should a Andy's a quiet boy. Hitt

I began developing definitions for bullying behaviors, roles children and adults assume in bullying situations, and effective ways of dealing with and supporting the bullies, the bullied, and the bystanders.

The Facts About Bullying

The consequences for bullied children can be devastating not only for them personally, but for the community at large. The question becomes not *if* we should do something, but *what* we will do to support our children. Here is a closer look at the problem.

At School and on the Playground

Bullying is so common in our schools that sometimes teachers, administrators, and support personnel disregard it. The American Academy of Child and Adolescent Psychiatry reports that "as many as half of all children are bullied at some time during their school years, and at least 10 percent are bullied on a regular basis" (www.aacap.org/publications/factsfam, 2003). A Canadian study (*The Journal of Psychology*, 2004) found that within a total school population, it's estimated that 10 percent are bullies, anywhere from 10 to 15 percent are bullied and the rest are "bystanders," a term coined by Barbara Coloroso in *The Bully, the Bullied, and the Bystander* (2003). Bystanders, those children who witness bullying, either join in or are unable to step in and stop the harassment.

Last week my daughter Kelly kept getting nasty text messages on her cell phone. You know the kind —"You're ugly," "No one likes you," "We're going to beat you up after school"—the mean things kids used to say to each other on the playground. But with the text messaging, we can't figure out who is sending them. I'm not technologically inclined, so how am I supposed play detective on Kelly's cell? How do I even get help with this? Kelly's sha...

I got a call from Logan's teacher this morning. She's accusing him of behaving like a bully. That just can't be true! Logan has lots of friends. He is such a leader that even the neighborhood kids do most everything he says, which is funny to see sometimes. I mean, Logan loves being in charge. How can that be a bad thing? Well, of course, it's a little different when he tries to boss his sister around and knocks her by mistake. Well, that's rights. Anyway, I

Bully or Victim: Labels or Judgments?

For the purposes of designating who is who and making this guide easier to understand, I've referred to some children as bullies, the bullied, bystanders, or victims. Those are labels with negative connotations and using them can be detrimental to a child's social and emotional growth and development, so please avoid using them with children. Just as a girl called a princess is inclined to act like a princess, so too is a child called a bully more resigned to play the part.

Instead of labeling your child, identify undesirable behaviors and/or call attention to his or her positive behaviors in order to build self-esteem. Consider the following statements and their implicit meanings.

• *Ayesha, there you go tripping other players! Why should I be surprised to see that you're such a bully on the soccer field?* (Labels Ayesha and in effect type-casts her as a bully.)

• *Ayesha, you tripped Otto on purpose during the game. Doing that was unkind and will likely make Otto reluctant to play soccer with you again soon.* (Acknowledges undesirable behavior and encourages Ayesha to imagine what it is like to be harmed. Encourages Ayesha to experience empathy for Otto.)

• *Ayesha, you tripped Otto. But when you helped him back up, Otto smiled from ear to ear. I bet he was glad to see that you still care about his friendship!* (Acknowledges undesirable behavior as well as Ayesha's efforts to replace those behaviors with caring overtures.)

For more information about the role of self-esteem, see page 47 in Chapter Three. If you're looking for ways to help your child develop empathy, turn to page 86 in Chapter Four.

Studies also reveal that while bullying intensity tends to increase in middle school, younger children are just as frequently bullied as older students (*The Journal of Psychology*, 2004). As parents, we may not realize that our children may be exposed to bullying at a much younger age than we were. Aggressive, bullying behavior can be seen in play schools and kindergartens—underscoring the importance of dealing with the issue with

> *"I think Ben feels there's no point in telling you." Ben's mother had said that Monday morning. "He tried to get help from you before, but he says Chad is still bullying him. He feels pretty hopeless."*

children in the early grades, before the behaviors become patterns and before the situation becomes dangerous.

Another survey, quoted by Kathy Noll, author and bullying expert (http://kathynoll.wordpress.com/bully-blog/), provides another startling statistic: every seven minutes, a child is bullied. In 4 percent of those situations adults intervened, peers intervened in 11 percent of the situations, and no intervention occurred in 85 percent of the situations. Those are astounding figures. Were the incidents seen by adults? These numbers confirmed what bullied children have been saying about lack of support.

Effects on Health and Wellness

With the prevalence of bullying in our communities and schools, it is no wonder that it takes its toll on children's physical and emotional health.

PHYSICAL HEALTH A recent study identified associations between bullying and common health problems in children. Researcher D. Wolke and his colleagues at the University of Hertfordshire in the United Kingdom studied 1639 children (ages 6 though 9). Their research found low to moderate associations between direct bullying, bullying that involved physical aggression (i.e., hitting) and health problems. Recommendations? If your child has repeated sore throats, colds, breathing problems, nausea, poor appetite, or school worries . . . talk with him or her and your child's physician about the possibility of bullying as a contributory factor.

[Adapted from Bullying Involvement in Primary School and Common Health Problems *(D. Wolke.)]*

MENTAL HEALTH Research also points to the psychological effects on bullied students who deal with the problem unsupported by family or other caring adults. In their book, *Bullycide: Death at Playtime* (2001), Neil Marr and Tim Field detail examples of children who have either been murdered by bullies, or who were so unhappy and tormented by bullies that they committed suicide. Their research looked specifically at bullying-related violence in the United Kingdom, where each year more than 16 children kill themselves.

While many bullied children turn their fear, frustration, and rage inward, some turn their anger into action. School shootings are a highly visible result of the toll bullying sometimes takes. The United States Secret Service released a report on preventing school shootings, saying: "In a number of cases, bullying played a key role in a child's decision to retaliate. A number of children had experienced bullying and harassment that were long-standing and severe. In those cases, the experience appeared to play a major role in motivating a retaliatory attack at a school. Bullying was not a factor in every case, and clearly not every child who is bullied in school poses a risk. However, in a number of cases, children described experiences of being bullied in terms that approached torment" (*Preventing School Shootings:* A Summary of a *U.S. Secret Service Safe School Initiative Report*, 2000, National Criminal Justice References Service, www.ncjrs.org/pdffiles1).

Most of us remember the tragic events of April 20, 1999, at Columbine High School in Littleton, Colorado, when two students went on a shooting rampage that left dozens of people wounded and 15 people dead (including the shooters, who committed suicide). The events brought attention to the bullying problem. (As a point of note, it has never been established clearly that bullying played a clear role in what happened.) The incident sparked reports and investigations, all looking for solutions to bullying in schools. A common thread emerged and was summed up well by Alicia Caldwell: " . . . while not every child pushed around in school is going to exact violent revenge, the abusive treatment of students by their peers is recognized not only as a widespread problem but a dangerous one" ("Columbine: A Recurring Nightmare," *Denver Post*, April 20, 2004).

Questioning Assumptions

Barbara Coloroso, author and parenting expert, writes: "Breaking the cycle of violence involves more than merely identifying and stopping the bully. It requires that we examine why and how a child becomes a bully or a target of a bully (and sometimes both) as well as the role bystanders play in perpetuating the cycle. A deadly combination is a bully who gets what he wants from his target: a bullied child who is afraid to tell; bystanders who either watch, participate in the bullying, or look away; and adults who discount bullying as teasing, not tormenting, as a necessary part of growing up, not an impediment along the way, as 'boys will be boys,' not the predatory aggression that it is" (2003).

Bullying: A Quiz

True or False?

❒	❒	Bullying is just a part of growing up.
❒	❒	Boys bully more often than girls.
❒	❒	Bullies don't usually have any friends.
❒	❒	Ignoring bullies often works.
❒	❒	If children fight back, bullies will leave them alone.
❒	❒	Bullies do poorly in school.
❒	❒	Bullies tend to be bigger physically than other children.
❒	❒	Bullies pick their victims indiscriminately.
❒	❒	Children who look different always become targets of bullies.
❒	❒	Bullies learn from parents who bully.
❒	❒	Name calling or teasing is not really bullying.
❒	❒	Kids who bully often feel sorry for hurting other children afterwards.

During my research on bullying issues, I grew more aware. I began reluctantly to see some of my beliefs reflected in Coloroso's statement. Didn't I really think that bullying is a part of growing up, and children should just learn to deal with it? Wasn't everyone teased? I came across many versions of quizzes relating to perceptions about bullying. Looking at my answers to those quizzes helped to open my eyes about my own assumptions and beliefs. To help you take a closer look at your own assumptions and beliefs, I invite you to take this quiz (page 16) that I developed especially for parents.

When, through my research, I came to understand that I had bought into many common misconceptions, I was startled. You might be startled too, to learn that ALL of the statements in the quiz are false! Before long, I found that I needed to change my whole approach toward children who bully, children who are bullied, and the children who stand by. I needed to know more about bullies: Could I predict who would be a bully in my classroom? What kinds of behaviors would be classified as bullying? Why did some children bully the same child repeatedly? There are many reasons why children bully others, and generalizing or making snap judgments about these children is neither fair nor reasonable.

Characteristics of a Bully

Children who bully come from many different socioeconomic backgrounds and family situations. They are influenced by examples of bullying and violence pervasive in television, movies, video games, and popular music. Bullies can exhibit behaviors that include physical and verbal aggression, taunts, threats, put-downs, social isolation, and the pretext of teasing. Bullies are children of all shapes, sizes, ages, and intellectual abilities. What they share is anger. Like many children (and adults), bullies find it difficult to express anger in appropriate ways.

> Bullying behaviors give power to one child at the expense of hurting, humiliating, or diminishing another child.

The ways they cope with the volatility of anger is problematic for their peers, their families, and sometimes the greater community.

While we may never completely eliminate bullying in our classrooms, schools, and communities, we can make a critical difference by giving our children the tools and skills that will help them feel more confident. We can help them learn to recognize a bullying situation and then act in strategic ways to solve the problem.

By dealing with this issue openly, and helping children realize that there are many options for dealing with bullies, we go a long way toward achieving our complementary goals—ensuring that all children feel safe and happy.

> **RESEARCH**
>
> **IN THE**
>
> Boys who were identified as bullies in middle school were four times as likely as their non-bullying peers to have more than one criminal conviction by age 24 (Olweus, 1993).

Dispelling the Myths

In his article "Bullying in Schools" (ERIC, spring 2000), Ron Banks dispels some of the myths about bullying. He found there is little evidence that bullies have low self-esteem. In fact, bullies tend to have overblown self-confidence and an exaggerated sense of self-worth. They are people who rely on aggression and power to control other children, children who are vulnerable—victims that "deserved it" or "asked for it" in some way. While some bullies have little interest in others' needs and find it difficult to take responsibility for their behavior, other bullies may struggle with clinical depression. And still more bullies have friends who tend to encourage and even emulate bullying behaviors.

Some children are perceived as bullies, even though power and dominance may not be their goal. Children with attention-deficit/hyperactivity disorder (ADHD) are often impulsive and may frequently exhibit behaviors that are irritating to others. They may not recognize that irritation and continue the behavior, not understanding the impact it is having on the other person. While children with ADHD may exhibit bullying behaviors, their behavior doesn't have as much to do with a desire for power as it does with an inability to respond appropriately to the social cues of their peers. That is, they simply are unable to "read" expressions or behaviors that people use to signal their feelings or intentions to others. Children with ADHD may resort to bullying, taunting, or aggression simply to get the attention of other children, hoping that somehow they will become part of a group.

Interestingly, a higher proportion of males than females are diagnosed with ADHD and a higher proportion of boys are thought to be aggressors. What's more, boys and girls have traditionally displayed different aggressive behaviors: Boys have tended to be more physically aggressive and violent. Girls have tended to bully verbally and socially; that is, they use exclusion, emotional abuse (taunting, starting rumors), and extortion. Recent reports and studies of violence by girls, however, may indicate that girls' aggressive behaviors may be increasing (Federal Bureau of Investigation, 2003, www.nationalsave.org/main/bully%20articles.php).

Formative Family Settings

According to British researchers Peter Stephenson and David Smith, bullies can be categorized into three groups: dominating bullies, anxious bullies, and bully victims (Sheras, 2002).

Dominating bullies tend to come from families that are rule-bound, with no room for discussion or compromise. Absolute power in a relationship is expected and children may come to feel that only the person who is in power will have their needs and wants met. And, of course, the sense of power that comes from forcing another to do something against their will gives the bully the validation and feeling of control that is so desperately craved.

Anxious bullies often come from the same type of family setting, but tend to have low

> **RESEARCH IN THE**
>
> **Bullies Who Were Victims**
>
> "Bully victims are considered the most potentially violent type of bully—the type to reach for a weapon or join a gang—because their rage is extremely high and their support systems weak. In other words, they are angry, in pain and all alone." (Sheras, 2002)

self-esteem. They tend not to initiate bullying events. Rather they take part in group bullying in order to gain acceptance within the group as well as protection from being bullied themselves. Anxious bullies are ruled by fear. Children who have been previously bullied often fall into this pattern.

Bully victims are children who have been victims themselves, and who try to make up for their abuse by bullying others. These bullies are often unsupported at home or at school, and have little guidance or sense that anyone cares for them. According to Peter Sheras (2002), studies show that the most common response to being a victim is anger, and the child takes out on others the anger about that abuse as he or she becomes the aggressor.

In Chapter Four, children who are bullies are the focus. There, various strategies and ways to get help are presented.

Characteristics of Bullied Children

It is often tempting for adults to blame the victim, to frame that bullied child as possessing a weakness, a perceived vulnerability that makes him or her especially prone to ridicule. However, children are targeted for many reasons. Rather than labeling them with stereotypes, we can identify some common characteristics of bullied children—and later, in Chapters Two and Three, we'll look at ways to empower those same children with coping skills and strategies.

Bullied children may:

♦ **appear vulnerable in some way.** They may be isolated from their peers and not have many friends, or be extremely shy, submissive, and timid. They may not read social cues effectively.

♦ **lack confidence in themselves in social situations.** They may be unsure of how to deal with others, and unable to stand up for themselves effectively.

♦ **have difficulty controlling their emotions**; they may cry easily or become extremely angry quickly.

♦ **exhibit behaviors that are annoying** to others at times, including talking excessively, having difficulty waiting for turns in games or group settings, and fidgeting or squirming when sitting (Thompson, 1996).

♦ **seem "different" in some way** (for example, ethnicity or physical disability). However, this difference tends not to be the only factor; lacking friends who will stand up for them, or exhibiting the characteristics mentioned above are much more crucial factors.

♦ **simply be in the wrong place** at the wrong time.

Of course, there are no acceptable reasons for children to be bullied. No one deserves to be harassed for any reason. However, the characteristics listed above shed light on the need for adults to help children develop confidence when dealing with bullies.

Social Bullying

Social bullying encompasses many forms of harassment and intimidation. It can sound like harmless gossip and classroom politics. When it is happening, it can look just like children engaged in conversation and gathered in pairs or cliques. It can be difficult to recognize, but it is no less destructive than other kinds of bullying. Susan Wellman, founder and president of the Ophelia Project, writes in the foreword of *My Secret Bully* (Ludwig, 2004) that emotional or "relational aggression," which is often talked about as a normal part of growing up, is in fact as harmful as physical aggression (page 1).

And now a new kind of social bullying is taking place on the Internet and via text messaging. Known as cyber bullying, this type of negative behavior often involves spreading rumors, issuing threats, and sometimes distributing negative graphics or pictures of the victim. This behavior is much harder to deal with because the violence is not physical but emotional, made more intense by the lack of face-to-face contact with the bully. Who is responsible for this? Who can I trust? There is no one to confront, and bullied children involved in this type of harassment may feel doubly unsafe.

Characteristics of Bystanders

Children who exhibit bullying behaviors do so in quiet, "under-the-radar-screen" areas. But more important, they are enabled by groups of children, called bystanders—children who are on the fringe of the bullying event. The bystanders may join in with the bully or may stand silently, unwilling (or unsure how) to help. How can we encourage bystanders to lend a hand to the bullied child and/or disempower the child who is bullying? In Chapter Three we'll look at how we can assist bystanders and encourage them to support a peer.

RESEARCH IN THE

A Secret Service report issued in 2000 indicated " . . . that in [one-half] of the school homicides examined, the attacker told someone about the planned attack, and in nearly all cases that person was a peer—a friend, schoolmate, or a sibling. They almost never told an adult." (Caldwell, 2004)

Conflict Versus Bullying

It's important to define the difference between bullying and conflict. Often the lines between the two are blurred, which reinforces the misconception that bullying is normal and children should toughen up and learn to deal with it.

Conflict occurs every day, and it is necessary for children to learn to sort out difficulties with others. Arguments over who owns the pencil or who cut in line are perfect examples. Name calling and teasing may be bullying behavior; however, it depends on the context. If children have equal status in a friendship, this can be part of normal horseplay. For children who are unequal in status (e.g., an older student with a kindergarten child, or a group of children teasing a solitary child), the same behaviors are bullying.

In a conflict situation, the behavior is often "made public" and easy to spot. For example, on the playground I saw that sixth-grade boys, in particular, delighted in jockeying for power. In those situations, whether they were play-fighting, teasing, or engaging in real conflict, it was obvious that the boys involved, and the children watching, all had relatively the same

In Action: Ginny and Vera

Once, during morning recess, a child came up to me to report that a group of girls were bothering another girl in her class. The incident was happening around a corner from where I was standing. As I rounded the corner, the girls saw me coming and quickly disbanded.

I was surprised to find that the ringleader was Vera, a girl I had taught previously and who had always been polite, easygoing, and friendly. Ginny, the girl being bullied, was a timid, shy, and quiet child who explained to me that Vera had been threatening to tell people a terrible thing about Ginny if she didn't move out of Vera's territory. It became clear to Ginny and to me that there was an unwritten rule on the playground—that a designated area belonged to the "gang" and Ginny had unwittingly strayed into the group's space. Ginny didn't know what the rumor was that Vera intended to tell. Nonetheless, Ginny was upset and stuck close to me for the rest of recess.

Later, after I had discussions with Vera and her followers (with me doing most of the talking), the girls made a reluctant apology to Ginny. As I watched the girls talking, I understood that those discussions and that apology weren't enough.

social status within the group; that is, they were usually friends who were matched up against each other and each boy was supported by friends. These "fights," even if serious, lasted briefly and usually took place in some visible spot. They tended to end if one person became really angry, or was hurt. Usually the boys were friendly afterward.

Bullying, however, often takes place out of sight of adults and *always* involves aggression and intimidation. It's an abuse of power, and the children who are targets are usually perceived as vulnerable. Most children go through times when they are bullied; in fact, it seems to be one of those universal experiences that humans share.

Children need to be able to distinguish bullying from conflict, they need to be able to feel comfortable telling an adult, and they need to be confident that they will be taken seriously and be given support and concrete strategies to help. Most of all, children need to realize that there are things they can do to stop the bullying and that they are not powerless.

They need to understand that the situation is not their fault, that no one deserves to be treated poorly, and that the feelings of shame they may have are not appropriate.

The Role of the Adult

How do adults fit into the picture? Ignoring the situation isn't the answer, but neither is stepping in and resolving the problem yourself. I discovered that setting consequences for children who bully helped me handle the situation temporarily, but took power away from the children who needed power most. In the role of "solver," I taught children little about handling the problem. If I solved a conflict that involved bullying, how would the bullied children develop the confidence they needed to stand up for themselves? When should I step in and when should I step back? After all, asking children to rely on an adult to come to the rescue may work at recess, but it is a pretty useless strategy on the way home from school.

A Road Map to Bullying

My research on bullying revealed layers of challenges that I would need to tackle to deal with the problem effectively, among them: How could I support bullied children, but at the same time help children who bullied?

To begin, I identified what bullied children need to defend themselves—specific, nuts-and-bolts strategies to use when they are bullied, positive ways to stand up for themselves, confidence in their abilities to problem-solve, and the knowledge that they deserve to be treated well.

Children who bully need to learn that there are benefits to dealing positively with other children. Bullies need to develop respect, tolerance, and, most important, empathy for others. They must also realize that there will be consistent and clear consequences for participating in harming others.

A lot of compelling information regarding bullying exists today and it can be overwhelming to get a sense of what to do or where to begin. The reality is that there are a variety of simple, basic things that children can do and many things you as a parent can do to begin to deal with and hopefully reduce or eliminate bullying altogether. In Chapter Two, we begin by focusing on children who are being bullied.

Truly successful decision making relies on a balance between deliberate and instinctive thinking.

~Malcolm Gladwell,
writer for The New Yorker

Before I was married I had three theories about raising children. Now I have three children and no theories.

~John Wilmot, Earl of Rochester
(1647–1680)

 CHAPTER TWO

What Can I Do to Help?

Children can be good at keeping painful secrets. In fact, some young children do not realize that they are being bullied, thinking instead that the bullying they endure is normal.

Is My Child a Target?

So how, then, can you tell whether your child is being bullied? There are many signs that children are being bullied. Those signs run the gamut from coming home with torn clothing to feeling sick and wanting to stay home to becoming quiet and withdrawn in daily life. Refer to the box on page 27 for additional warning signs.

If you suspect your child is being bullied, it is important to take some time to plan your actions and reactions. Your feelings of anger and hurt on behalf of your child will be strong. They may urge you to actions that have only short-term gains and may in fact make your child's problem bigger.

To react effectively, be proactive and think out what you might say or do. In this chapter, you are going to develop your own bully-proofing plan—a parental plan of action based on taking some time to reflect on

In Action: Me, the Author

I was a target of bullies in the seventh grade. Quiet and shy, I found myself a constant target in those difficult days of junior high. I tried hard to blend in with my surroundings, tried to laugh along with my tormentors, and struggled desperately to think of something that would stop the bullying. The one thing I didn't try was telling any adults.

Looking back on that time, I recognize a few truths about who I was, and wasn't. At the time I thought I was picked on because I was small and timid. It never occurred to me to stand up to the bullying; I never realized I had any power in the situation or could make different choices as to how I reacted. Because I saw few bullies held accountable for their actions, I felt that things would not change if I told anyone. I became convinced that I was a target for some reason I would never really understand. So, I decided simply to ride it out. Eventually, someone else became the target and I was left, for the most part, alone.

I did have a good friend, but she was, like me, unsure of the social complexities of junior high. We didn't dress in the latest fashions, and feeling unaccepted, shied away from the activities that popular kids enjoyed (like after-school clubs, sports, and parties). It was a lonely, confusing time. I see now that being small and out of the orbit of popularity were probably the least important factors in my being a target. My timidity, social isolation, and passive acceptance of the bullying likely made me an attractive target.

I didn't tell any adult about the bullying because I somehow felt it was my fault. I worried that the situation would disappoint my parents and felt apprehensive about any interference by adults. Would they be able to put a stop to it? Or worse, would their involvement intensify the bullying? When, as an adult, I eventually told my parents about my experiences, they were horrified. They felt terribly guilty about not knowing anything was wrong. Of course, now I know they would have supported me.

how you want to handle the situation and what you know about your own child. Most important, your plan will say to your child, "I hear you and I am taking you seriously, and this is what we will do if you are bullied."

If your child is not being bullied, creating a plan means you will be

Warning Signs—Is your child . . . ?

❏ Reluctant to go to school, the park, or other area

❏ Experiencing a sudden drop in grades

❏ Coming home hungry (missing lunch)

❏ Experiencing nightmares, wetting the bed, having difficulty sleeping

❏ Refusing to leave the home

❏ Waiting to get home to use the bathroom

❏ Acting nervous when an unfamiliar child approaches

❏ Showing increased anger or resentment with no obvious cause

❏ Talking about feeling lonely or about difficulty making friends

❏ Reluctant to defend himself or herself when teased or criticized

❏ Bruised, cut, or bearing scrapes that are not easily explainable

[Adapted from Your Child: Bully or Victim? *(Sheras, 2002)]*

setting your child up for success when he or she encounters bullying—whether it be as the bully, the bullied, or the bystander. Or, if your child has been bullied in the past, you may not be happy with how the situation was handled or resolved. Having a viable plan of action will help you and your child focus on strategies that will work more successfully.

My Child Is Being Bullied—What Next?

If your child tells you about being bullied, stay calm and go slowly! Instead of offering your advice right away, assure him or her that there are things you both can do to end the bullying. Set a time in the near future to come up with a plan together.

The first impulse of many adults is to step in, take over and solve the problem. It's tempting to call the bully's parents to demand an end to the behavior, march down to the school to demand that something be done, or advise your child to retaliate. While *some* of these options may be necessary later, the reality is that there will always be bullies and conflict in the world, on the playground, and in the workplace. Children need to be given the

My child just confirmed my suspicions. . . .
What do I say next?
"I'm really glad you told me. You know, this isn't your fault. I can see how much this has been bothering you. I've been bullied myself so I know how you feel. We are going to do something about this, but I want to think about the best way to help. How about we talk about this tomorrow night and come up with a plan?"

tools to deal with bullying behaviors, and you need to support your child by offering practical support. Adult-generated solutions rarely work. While solving your child's problem may be expedient and make you, as a parent, feel better, how will it help your child in the long run? How effective is a solution if your child comes to rely on adults to resolve his or her problems?

As you prepare to create your bully-proofing plan with your child, you'll find it a valuable experience to take some time to prepare yourself and to think about your personal parenting style and your beliefs about bullying. In fact, you can go through the exercise that follows anytime— even before problems occur. The questions are designed to help you focus on your strengths and think about the best ways to proactively support your child through a bullying situation.

SOME GUIDING QUESTIONS

- ♦ Examine your personal beliefs about bullying. What experiences do you have that may affect your thinking today?

- ♦ Look honestly at how you interact with your child. Do you feel you model respectful behavior for your children?

- ♦ What is your parenting style? If there is another active caregiver in your child's life, do you have similar parenting styles? How do you deal with differences of opinion when parenting?

♦ Take a look at how you talk with your child about issues he or she may be having. What kind of communication works? What doesn't work?

♦ Are the main caregivers in your child's life on the same page when it comes to bullying? How will you handle any disagreements about how to handle bullies?

♦ What resources may be available in your community? How will you access help from your child's school?

Examining Your Personal Beliefs

Developing an awareness of ways you relate to your child is an integral first step when thinking about supporting your child with bullying. It's also necessary to examine your personal beliefs about bullying and think about how these affect what you do today.

When I began to think about my attitudes toward bullies and bullying, I realized how much my bullying experience in seventh grade affected me. I am ashamed to admit that later, in junior high school, I became involved with a group of girls who bullied another girl. I can't explain why I took part, especially knowing how it felt to be the victim. I suppose I was just glad to be a part of the group—it made me feel powerful in a way I had never experienced before. Our victim did seek help, and a guidance coun-selor became involved. After a group discussion and apologies, we stopped the bullying behavior.

It's interesting to note that, with my bullying experience, when our target did get help, an adult stepped in and we stopped the bullying. Realis-tically, many children experiment with intimidating someone else, but stop when confronted with their behavior. This may be where the myth that bullying is a part of growing up comes from; however, it's important to reiterate that whether a one-time event or a repeated pattern of behavior, bullying needs to be dealt with.

This is not uncommon; many of us have been bullies and been bullied. What is interesting, though, is where this leads our thinking as adults— how our experiences can inform the decisions we make for and with our children. During my years of teaching, I looked back at the incident. I realized that I felt helpless when I was bullied, and I still felt helpless in the classroom when dealing with children who bullied. Why should I be surprised or frustrated that kids are reluctant to seek help? I was reluctant to seek help, too. I could also relate to being a bystander. When I took part in bullying in junior high, I was not the "lead" bully but joined in during the taunting. I was part of the group and I remember the sense of power and camaraderie (however false it may have been).

My experiences influenced how I dealt with bullies in my classroom. While I spoke to the children involved, I didn't know how to help children stop bullying. I knew how the act of bullying could fulfill a need to feel powerful. And I always felt frustrated and useless when most students continued their bullying behavior. How could I break that cycle when I knew the strategies and advice I offered bullied children was simply a variation on what I had tried myself in seventh grade . . . which was not helpful or successful?

Recognizing Your Parenting Style

Children who are treated disrespectfully cannot be expected to turn around and treat others properly. Those same children might feel that being bullied is acceptable because they deserve it in some way. (*If my parent treats me like that, it must be okay for others to do so as well.*) It is easy to forget that, as adults, we model all types of behavior unknowingly every day in our homes and beyond. It becomes essential for each of us to realize that the behaviors we demonstrate color the tone and effectiveness of the message we are trying to convey to our children.

Harsh, unreasonable consequences for behavior or, conversely, making excuses for your child's behavior, or dealing with problems emotionally and in a knee-jerk fashion, don't often lead to a positive resolution. Sarcasm, or disciplining publicly and with put-downs, devastates a child. Many of us remember having an adult who humiliated us publicly by making fun of us in front of others. And I have seen and heard parents today do the same thing to their children. Treatment like that diminishes both the child's dignity and the respect a child will have for his or her parent.

We need to align our words with how we act. It can be difficult when dealing with a child who has been repeatedly bullying your child (or when you're becoming frustrated with your child) to remember that *all* children need to be treated with dignity and respect. Parents are human beings. We become frustrated and angry. In the heat of the moment, it's easy to speak or act before thinking. But if we expect our children to speak respectfully, we have to ensure that we do the same. Even if it is difficult (especially when it is difficult), we need to take on our responsibility to model desirable behaviors.

A Parenting Style Spectrum

Just as we all have different beliefs and traditions, we also have individual parenting styles. It helps if you and your spouse have similar styles. If you don't parent in similar ways, it can be exasperating.

Barbara Coloroso defines three different styles of parenting: the brick wall, the jellyfish, and the backbone (in her books *Kids Are Worth It* and *The Bully, the Bullied, and the Bystander*).

In **brick wall families**, there are rigid rules, inflexible rules, and overly high expectations. There is repeated use of fear, sarcasm, humiliation, and, often, violence to maintain order and discipline. The parent is totally in control. He or she make decisions with little regard to the child's wishes or needs, and tells the child what to do and how to behave. When a child in a brick wall family has his or her ideas ignored or ridiculed, he or she begins to believe that in order to have power over others, he or she must have complete control—a characteristic ascribed to bullies.

Growing up in a brick wall family can be especially hard when children are not given the opportunity to deal with problems themselves and reason things through; they don't learn to trust their instincts, use their strengths, or develop the self-confidence they need to handle new situations effectively and appropriately.

> "From the outside, a brick wall family often seems to be a close-knit unit. But it is only a façade. Underneath the surface is a volatile mixture of anger, rage, degradation and frustration, held in place by brute force, coercion, or intimidation and waiting to explode—ideal conditions for creating bullies, vulnerable targets and reluctant bystanders." (Coloroso, 2002, page 84)

The predominant messages that brick wall parents communicate:

♦ I am in charge here, and your needs are not important.

♦ I will decide what is best for you.

♦ I have the power to control you and your behavior; therefore, you are powerless.

♦ I will not listen to your ideas, worries, or contrary opinions. Toughen up; emotions are not important in this family.

At the other end of the spectrum, one finds the **jellyfish families.** This style of parenting is free-form, with few (if any) rules, little discipline, and no consistency in terms of enforcing the rules that do exist. At times, discipline may be nonexistent. At other times, consequences may be harsh. Some jellyfish parents are concerned with personal issues and give little time or attention to their children. Other jellyfish parents may veer from frustration to panic when children become difficult to handle. A child's accountability for his or her own behavior is not viewed as important. Instead, the child's behavior is excused and blame is placed on other people or situations.

While some may believe that this "do what you like" household gives children the opportunity to develop freely, the structure (or lack of it) is actually frightening and difficult for children to navigate. They find it challenging to find their way when there are no boundaries to help guide their behavior and no safe haven to express their needs for help and support.

Children who come from a jellyfish family often have no context for how to behave, how to meet their needs appropriately, or how to survive in a world where others have needs that must be met. They are children who are often unable to gauge what is appropriate behavior because no one

> *When, because of self-centeredness, your view is narrowed to yourself, even a small problem will seem insurmountable.*
>
> ~HIS HOLINESS THE DALAI LAMA (2006)

shows them boundaries. In a sense, jellyfish families develop a culture of self-centeredness; children view the world only through their own wants and needs and are unable or unwilling to consider the needs of others. In their efforts to create an accommodating setting, jellyfish parents may believe (and hope) they are modeling tolerance and empathy. In reality, the opposite is true.

Children who have every need or wish met, who rarely are expected to follow rules or do things they don't want to do . . . are being short-changed in the long run. The "real world" is not kind to these children. Children who come from jellyfish families are easily frustrated and often over-whelmed. They simply have no experience or skills to react appropriately when others' expectations (such as coaches, instructors, and, later, man-agers) come into play. "Try, try, try again until you succeed" is a concept foreign to children who are used to getting their own way, children who—when the going gets tough—find coping difficult.

Often, jellyfish parents have come from brick wall families or jelly-fish/brick wall combinations. As adults, they have no idea how to create a safe, consistent environment for their own children. Instead, they tend to become overly involved in their children's lives, always there to rescue and eliminate problems—fearful of any situation that, in the parent's percep-tion, could be frustrating or harmful in some way to the child.

A version of jellyfish parents, **helicopter parents** continuously hover. They are ready to step in at any time to stand up for their child or resolve any problems the child may have. Helicopter parents mean well and love their children dearly. They are the parents who never realize how much they are actually hurting their children, never giving their children opportunities to learn how to deal

> "This panic and paranoia turns parents into Helicopter Parents, which is the most dangerous thing you can be for your child. If you are a fearful parent, you will raise fearful children. A scared, timid, nervous child is a great target, plain and simple." (Wilson, 2005)

with frustrations and other difficulties. Helicopter parents are, in effect, preventing their children from finding ways to resolve problems such as conflict and bullying.

In particular, helicopter parents may not realize that every time they step in and take over a task their child should handle, they send the message that they believe their child is weak, is not capable of dealing with a problem, and needs lots of help. Many parents don't realize that while our words send messages to our children, our actions and reactions speak volumes.

The predominant messages that jellyfish parents communicate:

♦ You can't predict what will happen in our family day to day.

♦ Do what you want; I may or may not notice and there may or may not be consequences.

♦ I will try and give you everything you want because it's easier for you (and me).

♦ I will take over and solve your problems for you because I don't think you are able to take care of yourself.

♦ If there's a problem, it's someone else's fault. You are not to blame, but don't do it again.

The final family style, **backbone parenting**, is built around structure, consistency, and clear expectations. Just as our backbones give us structure, they also enable us to be flexible. Backbone families demonstrate love and respect by their actions, and family members listen to one other and provide support. Children in these families feel they can ask for help, that they will not be ignored or belittled. Backbone families support the development of tolerance and empathy because they allow children to question, discuss, and experience many different situations. Because of clear boundaries, children feel safe and respected. That is, backbone families have rules; children experience the consequences for their behavior, and they are expected to take responsibility for their actions. Backbone parents offer suggestions and support, but their goal is to allow their child to learn and develop self-discipline and the confidence to deal with new situations.

The predominant messages that backbone parents communicate:

♦ I believe in you.

♦ I trust you.

♦ I know you can handle life situations.

♦ You are listened to.

♦ You are cared for.

♦ You are important to me.

(Coloroso, 2002, page 92)

Earlier, I discussed the importance of respecting all children, an idea that fits here as well. We must respect our children enough to allow them to experience life, with all its ups and downs, and let them muddle their way through. Of course, that's not to say that parents shouldn't support their children fully, but by making suggestions and offering guidance, these backbone parents allow their children to feel in control and confident.

Use the Parental-Control Continuum below to help you think about your parenting style. If your child is bullying others, you may need to closely examine what kind of behaviors you are modeling in your home, and what you may need to change or get help with.

If you are a two-parent household and you and your partner disagree on how to deal with issues such as bullying, you must sit down and discuss your concerns until you are both on the same page. Both parents must be united, talk the same talk and walk the same walk. It's essential to be united and support each other. Nothing confuses a child more than one parent who advocates beating the bully up, while the other supports non-aggressive ways of solving the problem. Resolve these differences before you move on.

A Parental-Control Continuum

Autocratic Style	Guidance and Boundary-Based Style	Permissive Style
"If I'm using the wheelbarrow, you stay back. That's the rule! That's what we're gonna do."	*"You can push the wheelbarrow after I dump the dirt. Thanks for waiting."*	*"Push the wheelbarrow, if you want. It's full and unsteady, so I'll try to keep it upright."*
BRICK WALL PARENTING	**BACKBONE PARENTING**	**JELLYFISH AND HELICOPTER PARENTING**

What Do You Do Now, and Does It Work?

Take a look at the suggestions and ideas you may be offering your child for handling bullies. Maybe you have a tacit agreement with your child about how to deal with bullying. Or do you have an explicit plan? As a classroom teacher, I just responded the best I could in each situation.

Sometimes my suggestions worked to end bullying. And maybe your child has had some success stopping bullying. If so, what was the key to his or her success? Are there strategies you've encouraged your child to try that haven't worked? And then, what would you like to see happen to the bully as a reasonable consequence of his or her actions? These are some of the questions and points of view you'll need to be considering as you move forward—looking for solutions to a bullying problem and building on the foundations of what is working for you and to the benefit of your child.

Making Use of Available Resources

Turn to a variety of sources for help and equip yourself with knowledge about bullying and how to stop it. In the Appendix you will find lists of the numerous books and videos I mention in this book. I've also included addresses of Web sites that offer information and support. If you need more in-depth help, particularly if your child is bullying others, ask at your child's teacher for recommendations and referrals. There are many places in our communities that offer help for families of bullies and bullied children, including local behavioral health organizations and police services.

Creating a Parental Plan of Action

You may feel overwhelmed when you realize your child is being bullied or is a bully; there is no gold-standard handbook for parenting in difficult situations. You may even be doubtful about your own parenting skills. But, never doubt that you know your child best. Remember, you are not alone and you *can* be a big part of the solution.

Having a plan, in any situation, helps give you a sense of control when or if things go askew. In this section, you will develop a personal bully-proofing plan—a "road map" with specific steps, detailing what you will do

> *The journey of a thousand miles starts with a single step.*
>
> ~CHINESE PROVERB

if your child is being bullied. This plan not only helps you feel confident that you will be able to deal with the problem in a positive manner, but it also helps your child feel comfortable. It shows him or her that you know what to do.

You may choose to have your child give some input on your bully-proofing plan of action. Or, you may prefer to collaborate on the plan with your spouse or other supportive adult (e.g., grandparent). If there are additional parental figures involved (e.g., stepparents), they need to be included in the planning as much as possible. If for whatever reason they do not take part in devising the plan, they should be given a copy and asked to cooperate for your son's or daughter's sake. And later, your child will have an opportunity to create his or her own plan of action. That plan will complement yours.

As awkward or as obvious as it may sound, your plan should be written down and positioned in a visible place. Written documents are important and meaningful in your child's world, making your plan that much more tangible and comforting. Write it on index cards or make a poster. Or do a fancy flowchart on the computer. What format will grab your child's attention and is appropriate for his or her reading level?

Go over the plan with your child, talking about what each step entails. When I did this in my classroom, the children commented that it was good to know that there was something active that I would do. They felt positive about knowing what would happen.

You must keep in mind (and remind your child) that your parental plan of action is not a one-size-fits-all plan. It needs to be flexible and have options. Life isn't set in stone—if one thing doesn't work, you must try something else until you find a solution that does not bring the victim down to the bully's level. (A flexible plan, does *not* include encouraging your child to beat up his or her tormentor. That tactic often backfires,

A Parental Plan of Action

To begin . . .

- Gather essential information from your child (e.g., who, what, where, when, bystanders, adult witnesses).

- Have your child record the details of what happened on paper. (Invite younger children to dictate while you write.) Save these notes for later reference.

* * *

Plan A

Scenario I:

Your child **knows the bully** *and* this is the **first incident**:

Step 1. Call the bully's parents and discuss the situation briefly.

- Invite them to bring their child to meet you and your child in a public spot that is conducive to quiet conversation (e.g., library, coffeehouse, diner). Note: If you feel it's necessary, invite a third person to mediate during the meetings, someone who knows both children (e.g., a coach, minister, teacher).

- Explain that you've had your child write (or dictate) an account of what happened. Encourage the bully's parents to have their child do the same and bring along the notes to the meeting. That way, both families will be able to compare notes.

Step 2. Meet with the bully's family.

- Meet with just the parents to discuss what happened and what should happen next.

- Have the children join the meeting and use the conflict resolution model (see Chapter Six).

- Invite your child to ask the bully for a letter of apology.

• Request restitution, if appropriate.

• Tell the bully's parents that you will follow up with them in a month's time.

Step 3. Talk about the meeting with your child.

• Review your child's bully-proofing plan and make modifications to meet your child's needs (see page 70).

• Role-play (current or new) strategies to use (see page 61).

Scenario II:

Your child **does not know the bully** *and* the bully is in your child's **school system:**

• Call your child's school to inquire about the bullying policy. Ask for support.

• Follow Steps 1 and 2. This time, invite a school administrator, guidance counselor, or teacher to act as the mediator.

• Follow Step 3.

* * *

Plan B

The bully continues to bully:

Step 1. Set up a meeting with the bully's family and a mediator. (Select a mediator both parties find suitable (e.g., school administrator, guidance counselor, or other go-between). As a group, develop an action plan that includes meaningful, clear consequences. Establish what steps each family will take if the bullying continues (e.g., involving a social services agency).

Step 2. Set up dates for follow-up conversations.

leaving your child in trouble and escalating the bullying.) At its heart, your plan should underscore that retaliation is not a viable solution, nor is any mean behavior or any kind of violence.

Use the suggestions on the template (pages 38 and 39) to guide you as you develop a course of action. (Is your child bullying others? You would create a different kind of plan, which is discussed in Chapter Four.)

Putting Your Plan Into Action

It's happened. Your child has come home and complained that a child has been bullying him or her on the walk home from school. Now's the time to create or review your Parental Plan of Action with your child, the time to take a deep breath and begin the process of supporting your child in a difficult situation.

Identifying What Happened

According to the model I've provided on pages 38 and 39, what you'll do next involves getting all the details and determining whether this is the first incident and whether your child is familiar with the bully. With those key pieces of information, you'll know whether to follow one of the scenarios in Plan A or whether to advance to Plan B. First, you'll want to help your

---

Discussion Prompts

Trying to have your child say more than "Greg was mean to me" can be a feat. To gather the responses you need in order to learn what really happened, try using one of these prompts.

♦ What would an instant replay of what happened look like?

♦ Describe what other people saw and heard during the incident.

♦ Why today? Why do you think he or she bullied you?

♦ What was the most frustrating part of the experience?

♦ If this happened again, what would you do differently?

child calm down and get all the details. Writing down the details helps your son or daughter focus on what actually happened. Young children, or those who have great difficulty writing, should dictate their ideas to you. Be careful not to coach ("You should say it this way") or add your own words. It is acceptable, though, to ask for more detail and to invite your child to clarify his or her thoughts. Your role is simply that of scribe. If your child has difficulty elaborating about the incident, you might try asking open-ended questions with the prompts listed on page 40. If your child is a reluctant writer, invite your child to write using the computer—whatever works! The goal is to have your child's version of events set down and in his or her own voice.

Plans A and B: Meeting the Bully's Family

Meeting with the bully's parents and/or caregiver should be part of any plan you develop. By meeting face to face with them prior to talking with the bully, you have an opportunity to discuss the problem frankly. Plus, it gives you all a chance to possibly circumvent problems that could otherwise crop up over time. Here are some items you should have available at the meeting:

♦ Writing tools for taking notes

♦ Your child's written account of the incident

♦ The bully's written account of the incident

♦ A copy of the reproducible template on pages 38 and 39 to help you navigate the process.

If you have any concerns about meeting with the bully's family, it may be wise to meet in a neutral place and have someone else join you to act as a mediator. Imagine how you would want someone to talk to you about your child if there was a problem and proceed from there. Remember that no one likes to hear unpleasant things about his or her child. Strong emotions, hostility, sarcasm, or personal comments about parenting should all be avoided during the meeting, even if the other parents respond in that manner. Don't be a bully yourself! Try and keep to the topic at hand and work toward an agreement as to how to proceed (conduct, possible consequences, restitution, or further action).

Meet with the bully's parents to start, while the children occupy themselves with books, drawing, toys, and so on. Ask for a volunteer to take notes about what is said and what is decided, and to make sure each family receives copies afterward. This documentation is essential in that it highlights the importance of the situation—you are taking things seriously. After you've talked with the bully's parents for a few minutes, invite the children to join the meeting. Ultimately, your aim is to have the children resolve their issues collaboratively. This can be made easier with the support of their families, who are in close proximity and who are encouraging them verbally and nonverbally (a hand on the shoulder, a nod, and so on).

Have each child read his or her account of the situation (no interruptions from anyone) and then go through the conflict resolution steps. Make sure each child is given time and the opportunity to speak. Keep all the parties involved on topic. When ready, ask the children to give input about the consequences they believe will be fair (it amazes me how realistic and reasonable children can be when they are expected to come up with resolutions). The children may readily have solutions to the bullying. If not, or if their ideas are not practical or possible ("sending the bully to Mars" would fit into this category), you will offer the ideas you as parents have discussed. Remember, you are trying to work together with the other parents to resolve the problem; listen to their ideas and wishes as well. While you may talk about applying consequences, ultimately it is not your decision to make. It is vital for both children to choose from the ideas that have been put forward and agree on the one they will try.

Plan A: Challenges and Outcomes

First-time problems are usually fairly simple to resolve. The bully should be sincere in his or her apology and willing to make restitution if needed and possible. Restitution, according to Barbara Coloroso (2002), "... means fixing what you did." Damage to personal property, stealing lunches, and so on can be relatively simple to fix. Other forms of bullying may not be as easy to deal with, other than having the bully make a personal pledge—that is, to be specific about how he or she will behave if and when there is a next time. If a child needs prompting or if the incident involves an older child, have him or her write a pledge on paper. Then ask each child to sign it. Again, having a document lends credence to the pledge itself. Plus, sending copies home with each family imparts a feeling of commitment to the resolution process.

Aim to have the meeting end on a positive note by acknowledging each child's courage and participation in dealing with a difficult situation. It is not easy to face your tormentor or your accuser. Children and parents need to feel proud of their efforts and willingness to take on the bullying.

Plan B: Challenges and Outcomes

Sometimes a bully and/or the bully's parents don't take bullying seriously. In this case, meet with the family and an outside person to act as mediator, someone who has authority and whose presence will underscore both the seriousness of the bullying and the expectation that it will stop. As a group, develop an action plan that includes meaningful, clear consequences. If the bully's family declines to participate in the process, you may need to involve outside resources, such the police department.

While you cannot control the bully's behavior, you can provide opportunities for your child to be given specialized help and support to deal with the bullying. You can access help by speaking to your doctor, school counselor, social services worker, or minister. Your school district will likely have supports and resources in place to help (even if the bullying does not take place at school). Plus, your local behavioral health associations may have information available as well.

Most bullying problems will be resolved by following your Parental Plan of Action consistently, and by not stepping back or avoiding the issue. When bullies (and their parents) realize you and your child will hold them accountable for their behavior, most will stop the bullying. When your child realizes he or she has power and can control the situation to some degree, he or she will feel more capable in bullying situations. When your child sees your support and recognizes that you know what to do, he or she will feel comfortable telling you about problems.

Most important, the confidence that *you* have in your ability to support your child during crisis—is contagious. It will go a long way toward helping your child develop strong bully-proofing skills he or she can use in the future.

In Action: Ben and Chad

As I've mentioned, I had a bully-proofing classroom plan that was similar to the Parental Plan of Action you've been developing. This is how my classroom plan looked "in action."

Chad was at it again. Ben came into the classroom with a tear-stained face and his shirt askew. I quietly pulled him aside and heard a by-now familiar tale. Chad had chased him, pulled on the back of his shirt, and then stolen his recess snack.

Ben and I talked about what had happened, and I reassured him that the bullying he was experiencing was not his fault. I told him that I knew that he and other children in the class were having trouble with bullies, and we were going to do something about it. With that, I pulled out my Personal Bullying Plan, and showed Ben the steps we would go through to try and resolve this problem. Once he could see that I was going to do something, he looked quite hopeful.

Next, I met with Chad during library time, and got his side of the story. As I expected, he felt Ben had provoked him because he had run away when Chad had "just gone over to see what he had for a recess snack."

Interestingly, when I asked Chad to tell me what a bully was, he couldn't seem to link his own behavior with the examples of bullying he gave me. Bullies, to him, were always older children who kicked you and made fun of you. He was quite taken aback when he heard the definition of a bully, and when I showed him my Personal Bullying Plan, he began to realize that I was going to hold him accountable for his behavior, and that there were going to be consequences for him.

Because Chad and Ben were in second grade, I had them write a brief version of what had happened. When the two boys came together, first Ben read his description and then Chad read his. While the boys disagreed on many points, there were similarities in both versions, and Chad grudgingly admitted that, yes, some of the things Ben said were true and he had "forgotten" to write those parts down. Ben had the opportunity to describe to Chad how he felt when he was being harassed, and he told him what he wanted Chad to do the next time they were outside at recess.

"Chad," Ben said, "you always take my recess snack, and that really hurts my feelings and it makes me mad, too. If you just ask me, maybe I'll give you some, unless it's my favorite."

Chad looked thoughtful. After both boys had said everything they felt they needed to say, I sent Chad off to think about an apology. I introduced the idea of restitution, and wondered out loud how he could fix what he had done.

After school that day, Chad delivered an apology note that was decorated with some small pictures showing Ben giving Chad some of his snack. As restitution, and without any prompting, Chad suggested that he bring a snack for Ben the next day. And he did.

While things worked out, I didn't believe for a moment that Chad had entirely reformed; it was, however, a successful first step. After that, Chad's bullying of Ben diminished, and by the end of the year, while not close friends, they got along and no further support was needed.

Keeping Useful Records

As you work through your Parental Plan of Action, keep records of the specific steps you've taken. Create a place (e.g., a folder) where you can keep copies of your plan along with any information you've gathered. This is also a good place to store the transcript of your child's account of the incident, notes from phone conversations and face-to-face meetings, notes from the school (if involved), a copy of the bully's pledge, and anything else you feel is important for future reference.

This documentation may be indispensable if the bullying continues and your family needs to access outside help. Plus, having your records at the ready and being able to refer to them easily lets others know that they are accountable for both their words and actions. If there is a question about who said what, or who agreed to what action, this material will be worth its weight in gold.

Involving Your Child's School

Working with your school is another component of bully-proofing, even if the incident occurred off school property. It is helpful for you to establish a relationship with your child's teacher and administration before problems arise. Teachers can be valuable allies and may offer support or ideas that can help.

Ask your principal for your school's bully-proofing policies and plans. If you feel it is appropriate, share your personal plan with him or her. If you are going to be asking for support during a bullying situation, make sure that your child's teacher and the principal have a clear idea about what you plan to do and what you expect them to do to help.

Many teachers and principals will be more than happy to work with you. It is reasonable to expect their support, whether or not the bullying takes place at the school or in the community. Be aware, however, that the school is limited in its ability to become involved when it takes place outside of school property or hours. Schools must follow confidentiality policies and structures set in place by the school board. They are not bound to supply you with the names, phone numbers, or additional information (such as previous bullying incidents) of other children involved. It may be appropriate for you to request that your name and phone number be passed to the other parents to initiate communication.

If you are working with the school to deal with a problem that happened at school, be sure to maintain a paper trail. Don't assume that the school will do so. Keeping useful records will again be invaluable if you need to move farther up your school district's administrative chain of command.

I was brought up to believe that how I saw myself was more important than how others saw me.

~Anwar el-Sadat,
former president of Egypt

Nobody can make you feel inferior without your consent.

~Eleanor Roosevelt,
former First Lady of the United States

©Maria Sweeney/Gettyimages

 **CHAPTER THREE**

Bully-Proofing

If you're thinking about talking with your child about bullying, it's also the time to become more aware of the importance of his or her self-esteem. Children who are confident, who can take risks, and who have parents who support them with constructive comments are children who can handle problems appropriately. A child who says, "I can't, I'm so stupid, I'm such a dummy" lacks confidence and is vulnerable to bullies. But how do you help your child develop the confidence and self-esteem that are so critical?

Self-Esteem and Confidence

All children (and adults!) go through times when they feel unsure of themselves, but when a child consistently demonstrates unhappiness or puts himself or herself down, it's time to take stock and deal with those feelings. It's time to look around for footholds on which to build self-esteem and confidence.

In Action: Rex

Seven-year-old Rex was tentative and unsure of himself when handling new situations. He would often refer to himself as a "dummy," mutter that he wouldn't be able to do a new activity, or give up on unfamiliar or challenging work when he was overwhelmed. Socially, Rex didn't have a "best" friend in his class, preferring to hang around on the fringes of an activity. This lack of confidence and uncertainty about friendships was also having an effect on Rex's view of himself as a likeable, competent person.

Rex's parents were facing a situation most parents face on occasion: When your child has a negative self-image, what do you do? His parents were frustrated by his continued put-downs of himself and poor self-image. They were pleased with his academic progress but could see that he didn't seem to be absorbing their positive messages. *He* didn't feel successful.

A Knack

Think about what your child feels really confident about. Does he or she have a special ability? Some skill that he or she is really good at? The talent doesn't have to be academic. It can be related to arts, sports, or anything that a child loves and feels good about. The goal here is to add another base on which to build your child's confidence in general. When a child feels successful, it gives him or her the feeling of being capable. And when one feels competent, one can handle new things—it becomes easier to face new challenges . . . and bullies.

Responsibilities

Another simple way to help children feel worthwhile and capable is to ensure they have consistent responsibilities around the house. Yes, the dreaded "c" word: chores! While you may not be enthusiastic about getting into a battle about taking the garbage out, the reality is that having responsibilities will increase your child's sense of competence. Doing chores involves expectations. Your child needs to know that the family will rely on him or her to do tasks that are relevant.

So, if Rex is expected to set the table for dinner every night, and he forgets (or resists), his parents sit down at the empty table and wait for him to set it. No dinner 'til the table is set! Rex needs to see that his contribution is essential. His parents won't rescue him. The role of the chores and your enforcing them will ultimately have an impact on Rex's overall view of himself. When he sees himself as a competent, responsible person, it will make him less vulnerable in general and to bullies in particular.

> *Self-efficacy* is the idea that if you've met challenges in the past, you can meet challenges in the future.
>
> "[For that reason] . . . developing a competency of any kind strengthens the sense of self-efficacy, making a person more willing to take risks and seek out more demanding challenges." (Goleman, 1995)

Praise Versus Encouragement

Helping a child feel positive and good about himself or herself is not simply a matter of praising each positive thing he or she does. In fact, over time, praise that is given by rote rather than for something truly earned becomes meaningless. Praise the behavior you see that is working. Be specific. "Wow, good job . . . way to go" is a glib way to praise someone without really thinking about it. "Wow! You swam four laps without stopping! Your swimming is really improving" is much more meaningful. Also avoid rewarding accomplishments with things like stickers, treats, and special activities. Your child's reward is feeling good about himself or herself as a person.

In Action: Rex

Rex's parents had observed that Rex tended to be a bit of a loner, so up to that point they hadn't tried to get him involved in many other activities. They felt it would be counterproductive to push Rex into joining an activity he wasn't interested in. Since Rex loved to read, they looked for a book club or library program he could join. Since he liked to bake cookies, they looked for programs that offered cooking lessons for kids. In short, they decided to provide Rex with some new experiences and opportunities to meet other children within his interest and comfort zone.

Children who don't take risks or find success at something (hitting a baseball, learning new dance steps, solving a difficult math question) need support and encouragement to continue trying. *I believe in you. I know you are doing your best. If you keep trying you will get this.* These are crucial messages! Children know when they have truly succeeded at something. They also know when they are being praised for the wrong reasons.

Talking About Bullying

A child who is confident is more likely to be interested in talking about bullying and what he or she can do about the problem. Talking with your child about bullying begins the bully-proofing process.

It is best to start talking to your child about bullying *before* there is a problem, but it's not always something you can plan. Either way, your child needs to gain a clear understanding of what bullying is and what he or she can do about it. These talks form the basis for learning the Top Ten Strategies for Handling Bullies, which are presented later in the chapter (page 61).

Starting the Conversation

How should you begin to talk about such a large and potentially frightening issue? Your main goal is to present information in a positive way and to set aside lots of time to talk about and explore the ideas you will present.

Discussing bullying is a little like peeling an onion—there are a lot of layers (issues) that come up and a few tears may be shed as experiences are revealed.

If you have more than one child, you should decide which discussion will include everyone and which will be more appropriate for individual children. If possible, both parents should be involved in each discussion, especially since the strategies and plans you come up with need to be understood and supported by each parent. Again, issues about the best way to resolve bullying problems need to be sorted out between you and your partner in private and before you broach the subject with your children. As the parents, it is essential that you both walk the same walk and talk the same talk.

Set for Success

Plan for times you will sit down with your child and talk about bullying. It's tempting to think that you will find unscheduled times to get together, but the reality of daily life is such that often the day goes by before you know it. Book times in your personal or family calendar. Once a week is manageable for most families, unless the bullying situation is current or ongoing or more talks seem to be needed. Give yourself at least a half-hour so the discussion can feel relaxed and unhurried as your child learns with you. And bear in mind that younger children may need briefer, less intense sessions to process all the information you discuss.

Minimize distractions. Choose a spot to talk that has no televisions, MP3 players, or computers. Let your phone take messages. Creating such an environment communicates to your child that he or she is the most impor- tant thing at that moment and *nothing* will be allowed to interrupt you.

Some of the discussions you have with your child may result in making lists (of bullying behaviors, people who could help, and so on), drawing pictures, or creating other records of your ideas or decisions. Visuals like these are really important for you and your child. They offer a reminder of what you have discussed and actions your child should take. You can use ordinary poster paper, computer paper, and colorful writing tools to address the bullying problem creatively. Then, position the results where your child can easily see the results of your conversation about bullying. If you choose not to extend your discussions into making visuals, your children will still benefit. You may just need to revisit your conversation more often to reinforce the concepts you've covered.

Taking a Look Around

Using your child's observations (from books, television, etc.) can be a helpful springboard for easing into the topic of bullying. When you notice an example of bullying behavior, examples of conflict, or inappropriate ways of solving problems (using violence, and so on), mention it to your child. Look around you for examples of people who do solve problems with others in appropriate ways.

Having a shared experience with your child (e.g., watching people at the park engage in conflict) can also help let him or her know that it isn't only children who can be bullied. You might discuss why you think an incident could be classified as bullying instead of just conflict. Talk about what you would have done to resolve the bullying. You may want to talk about times you were bullied and what you did about it. Listen when your child tells about times he or she saw others bullied or experienced it first-hand. How did your son or daughter feel? What did he or she do to stop the bullying?

Sharing books is a down-to-earth way to begin talking about bullying issues. It is important that the books you choose reflect your discipline philosophy and take into account the bully's perspective. Many storybooks and advice books about bullying offer solutions at the expense of the bully. There are many ways to deflect a bully that don't involve nastiness. Sarcastic comments and cruel tricks may make a funny story, but the lessons they teach are troubling ones. Meeting aggression with more aggression, humiliation, or sarcasm reduces the bullied child to the same level as the bully. If we expect our children to be respectful and maintain the dignity of others, we need to make sure that our solutions to bullying respect the child who is the bully, however challenging that may be.

Using Books

To help you find positive stories you and your child can read together, I've included suggestions of what books to read and when. I've also included recommendations for activities you can do with your child that support many of your shared bully-proofing goals.

The books mentioned in the Recommended Reading sections of this guide can be readily found in libraries, bookstores, and on the Internet. If

 Recommended Reading

WHY: To initiate a discussion about bullying

READ: *Bailey the Big Bully* by Lizi Boyd

In *Bailey the Big Bully*, the character Bailey torments others in his class until Max arrives. Max isn't going to be pushed around and he stands up to Bailey. Although the adults provide little support and Max resorts to punching Bailey (he is disciplined for doing this), the story demonstrates some appropriate ways of dealing with bullies. Max and his friends try to show Bailey ways to be a friend. They reach out to include him in their activities, and the story is resolved in a positive way.

After reading, ask how your child knew Bailey was a bully. Record a list of the behaviors that would be classified as types of bullying: physical, social (bullying within friendships, such as exclusion), verbal (put-downs, taunts, name calling, starting rumors), and other sorts of intimidation (threats, making someone do something, extortion). You may need to change or soften the language to be age-appropriate. Take time to list examples of behavior that would fit in each category. Is teasing a way to bully someone? What about laughing at someone? As you add things to the list, you may need to steer the discussion and include behaviors that were not mentioned in the book.

ALTERNATIVE: *Nobody Knew What to Do* by Becky McCain

Sensitively written and illustrated, this tells the story of a boy who is being bullied and the reaction of another boy who sees and reports it. Teachers, the principal, the parents, and students are all included in the solution. You could link the solution in this story to your Parental Plan of Action and reiterate that everyone needs to work together to end bullying.

for some reason you can't access the books discussed, mention your interests to a librarian at your local library or at school. Librarians can often track down similar books on the subject. They can also suggest substitutions that are on topic for you and age-appropriate for your child.

As you talk about a book with your child, keep your discussion focused on the topic of bullying and what the two of you learn from the story. It is important, too, to find an appropriate place within your discussion to introduce (or reiterate) the definition of a bully:

> **A bully is a person who threatens, scares, or hurts other people so they will do what the bully wants.**

To give your discussion some closure, invite your child to draw a picture about the story, what bullies do, or a time he or she was bullied. For an older child, invite him or her to write or draw in a journal or notebook set aside for that purpose. This will provide your child with a few minutes to process the story and the discussion you had about it. Your son or daughter will make important inferences about the story that he or she can later draw on.

Book Discussion Tips

There are a few tricks to getting a good discussion going about a book you've read. (Of course, it's essential that you read the book first—before you read it with your child.) When you begin, it is often tempting to ask question after question, a kind of Spanish Inquisition. Ugh! Asking too many questions becomes boring and tends to turn children off.

◆ Focus on one or two points in the story that you think are the most important. Asking open-ended questions helps spur conversation and gives you an idea about whether your child truly understands the concepts in the story, relates the story to his or her own experience, and is able to put together what he or she knows to come up with ideas for solutions.

◆ As you talk about the stories you share, try and relate your child's experiences (or your own experiences) to what happens in the book. When children hear stories from your life, it accomplishes two things. First, all children are entertained by the exploits and experiences of their parents. Second, they are reassured that you understand what they are feeling if you have been in that situation also. If your response to being bullied was not successful, share that saga. If you used a method that now goes against your philosophy (for example, beating up the bully), it's a perfect time to talk about that, too.

Open-Ended Questions

These are questions that allow for more than one response (more than a yes, no, or factual answer). As such, open-ended questions give your child room to elaborate on what he or she is thinking. What's more, they can help your child draw connections between reality and fiction. Here are some prompts you can use to get you started:

• I wonder what would have happened if . . . .

• What could (the character) have done after _____ happened?

• What makes you think what they did was a good choice?

• What do you think might happen the day after the end of this story?

• If this happened to you, what would you choose to do?

Nonviolent Solutions

Many adults talk about solving their own bullying problems long ago by beating up the bully or about being coached to react physically. While these solutions may have worked then, it's a different world today than it was even five years ago. Using aggression or violence can result in a different outcome. As a parent, be prepared to talk about whether or not beating someone up really worked. For some it might have, but more often the bullying continued. Discuss why aggression is a dangerous strategy for your child to adopt. The "I did it but don't you" line is not hypocritical when lawsuits, school expulsions, and weapons have become a common way of reacting to problems with others. Talking about using nonviolent ways of dealing with bullying is important. Furthermore, it's a great lead-in to a discussion about the Top Ten Strategies for Handling Bullies (page 61).

Conflict or Bullying: What's the Difference?

You may have discovered that your child doesn't have a good grasp of what bullying is and how it is different from normal, everyday conflict that we all encounter. Understanding the differences between them is a skill you need to help your child acquire.

To help your child learn more about what conflict is and what it looks like, gather a few familiar books or DVDs that you and your child have shared. Include a comic book or two, if you think they'll add to the discussion. Start off by asking your child to think about ways in which conflict is around us every day. Next, together look at the materials you have gathered and decide on the main conflict within each story. (All fiction has some form of conflict.) Then offer a definition of the word *conflict* and ask your child to tell you some examples that support that definition.

After establishing what conflict is, work together to define the difference between bullying and conflict. For help with identifying some major differences between them, turn to the reproducible chart on page 57. Add your own ideas to the chart if you'll find them helpful.

Take the time to talk about the fighting issue. Stress that people get angry and that's okay, but physical fighting and hurting others is not okay. Go back to *Bailey the Big Bully* (see page 53). Max hit Bailey and Max was the one who got into trouble. Hitting Bailey didn't solve the problem. Talking out conflict is always the best way to go.

For further practice on differentiating between conflict and bullying, read aloud some of the scenarios on page 57. Ask your child to listen carefully and then identify which scenarios fit the description of conflict and which seem more like bullying situations. Discuss each scenario. If you find your child has difficulty identifying the distinctions, repeat this activity in a few weeks' time. It's practice in the safe setting of your home that will help solidify your child's grasp of each type of situation.

> Conflict happens when people disagree about something or have ideas that are incompatible—and have trouble resolving the issue. Usually, the problem is worked out, and people are friends again. Not cleaning your room when I ask you to, arguing with your brother, and disagreeing over whose night it is to take out the garbage . . . are all examples of conflict.

Conflict or Bullying?

Use these scenarios to help your child learn the difference between conflict and bullying.

| CONFLICT | Sally and Emma are sitting on the swings. Two boys come over and ask them for a turn on the |

swings. Sally says no, and goes on swinging. The boys are angry and start yelling at the girls. The boys go off to find a teacher.

| CONFLICT | Rafael is missing his favorite pencil. He suddenly sees Brandon using it. "Hey, give me back my pen- |

cil!" he yells. Brandon tells him he found it on the floor and now it's his pencil. Rafael takes Brandon's eraser and throws it into the garbage can.

| BULLYING | Three boys are in the boys' bathroom. They start throwing wet paper towels all over the floor and |

laughing. A boy from another class comes in to wash his hands after art. The three boys start throwing wet paper towels at him. When he tells them to stop, they threaten to go and tell his teacher he threw the towels. They tell him to pick up the mess, or else. Then one boy kicks him in the leg.

| BULLYING | A group of girls in third grade have been friends since first grade. One day, Susan tells the other |

girls not to be friends anymore with Camille. The other girls agree, and run away from Camille at recess and lunch. They won't tell her why, and Camille starts to cry because she doesn't know why they are doing this to her.

| BULLYING | On the way home from school, Sean is chased by the biggest boy in his class, Steve. Steve pulls him |

behind a garbage can, and tells Sean to bring him a recess snack tomorrow. Steve threatens Sean and tells him if he knows what's good for him, he'll do it.

| CONFLICT | Mikhail likes to play soccer, but Jordan plays rough. Mikhail tries not to play when he's there. |

During one game, Jordan tripped Mikhail and tore his pants.

The Inclinations of Bullies

By now, your child should have a clear understanding of the differences between bullying and conflict. He or she is ready to think about children who are bullies. By helping your child develop an awareness of how bullies find children to target, you can help him or her feel empowered—empowered enough to make plans about how to react to a bully.

If your child tends to be someone who turns inward, take time to reassure him or her that a person can be shy and still stand up for himself or herself. Talk about why bullies target some people and not others. Explain that some bullies have common attributes.

Bullies like to pick on:

♦ people who don't stand up for themselves

♦ people who are quiet and won't tell on them

♦ people who are on their own, away from other kids or adults

♦ people who get upset easily or cry

Bullies don't like:

♦ people who say "no!" in loud voices

♦ people who feel confident and can handle problems

♦ people who tell and get help

♦ people who play in groups and include everyone in games

Dealing With a Bully

What really works to stop a bully? As a first step to answering this question, your child needs to think about successful ways he or she can react to a real-life bully. To help your child determine what responses to a bully are positive, try the activity on page 60, Reacting to a Bully.

Discuss in detail each scenario on the page. Stress that there is no "magic strategy" that always works when dealing with a bully.

Recommended Reading

WHY: To illustrate the power of self-confidence and empowerment

READ: *Mean, Mean Maureen Green* by Judy Cox

(*Note: Because this book is 83 pages long, you may want to begin reading it the day before or break it into sections to be read throughout the day. You'll need to finish reading the story before doing the activities below.*)

In *Mean, Mean Maureen Green,* the main character, Lilley, is terrified of Maureen, an older girl on her bus. Lilley is timid and calls herself a wimp when she fails to stand up to Maureen. A new boy, Adam, arrives and is not fazed by Maureen at all. (In fact, he plays a cruel trick on her and implicates Lilley.) Lilley sees how Adam handles Maureen but is still unable to do anything about the bullying herself. She decides to solve the problem by finally learning to ride her bike (rather than take the bus). She encounters other scary situations along the way, including an encounter with a vicious dog. As Lilley feels more confident being able to ride her bike, though, an unexpected encounter with Maureen helps her realize that she can handle the bullying situation. The issue with Maureen is not clearly resolved at the end, but Lilley sees things with a fresh perspective.

After reading the book, discuss the relationship between Lilley and Maureen. Was Lilley being bullied or was this conflict? What evidence is there? Who was rude first? How did Lilley feel when she saw Maureen? How do you think Maureen felt when she saw Lilley? Do you think that Lilley deserved to be treated like that by Maureen? Why or why not? If there is any uncertainty about whether this was bullying, refer to your list of types of bullying and relate the events in the story to the chart (page 57).

ALTERNATIVE: *Stand Tall, Mary Lou Melon* by Patty Lovell

Bullies don't like powerful children. Mary Lou Melon "is short and clumsy, has buck teeth and has a voice that sounds like a bull-frog being squeezed by a boa constrictor." But she has a wonderful grandmother who supports her ("Walk as proudly as you can and the world will look up to you."). Mary Lou does this well until, at her new school, she is tested by a bully named Ronald Durkin. Mary Lou Melon may be small, but she exemplifies the message you want your child to hear—being confident and happy with yourself makes you one smart cookie. (Discussion about Mary Lou's troubles also provides a neat segue into the Top Ten Strategies for Handling Bullies [page 61].)

Reacting to a Bully

Read aloud each scenario. Ask your child to identify whether the bullying was handled in a positive way or a negative way, or whether it could have been handled better. Discuss the suggested answers and explanations provided.

- **A bully calls you a name and you say in a loud voice, "Stop that. I don't deserve to be treated like that." Then you walk away.** (POSITIVE—Bullies don't like people standing up to them and using loud, assertive voices.)

- **A bully steals your hat and you start to cry.** (NEGATIVE—Some bullies like to make people cry and may continue to see how upset they can make you.)

- **A bully is walking over to you, so you look down and hunch your shoulders so the bully won't notice you.** (NEGATIVE—This makes a person look scared and easy to push around.)

- **A bully steals your recess cookies, so you hit him and try and get them back.** (NEGATIVE—Hitting him means you'll probably be the one who gets into trouble, and if the bully decides to hit you back, you may get hurt.)

- **A bully has been calling you names and laughing at you, so you tell your friend.** (POSITIVE—Telling a friend is a good start because they can help stand up for you. It would be even better if you told your teacher or another adult, so they could help, too.)

- **A bully keeps tripping you when you are playing soccer. You say loudly, "Stop tripping me. I want to play soccer, not fight with you."** (POSITIVE—Bullies often don't want others to know they are bullying people, and your friends on the team may stand up for you.)

- **A bully is standing over behind a tree and calls for you to come over. You walk away from the bully toward a group of people on the playground.** (POSITIVE—Bullies like to use out-of-sight places to bother people, but being near other people means the bullying will be seen if it continues. Besides, you don't have to do anything a bully tells you to do!)

- **A bully pulls you into an alley and threatens to beat you up unless you give him your jacket. You yell, "Help!" as loudly as possible and run as fast as you can to a place where there are other people.** (POSITIVE—If you feel you are in a dangerous situation, running is a good choice. If you yell "Help!" people are more likely to come to your assistance.)

- **A bully makes fun of your haircut, and so you make a funny joke about his or her hair.** (COULD BE BETTER—Sometimes a funny comment can defuse a bully, but be careful not to make fun of the bully. Putting down someone else or making fun of that person makes you as bad as the bully.)

- **A bully is telling your friends not to play with you at recess, so you go and join another game with other people in your class. Then you go home and tell your mom.** (POSITIVE—Walking away and joining in another game shows the bully and your friends that you won't be treated badly and that you have other friends. Telling your mom is a great idea because she can help you learn even more bully-proofing strategies.)

- **A bully is making your life so miserable you pretend you're sick so you can stay home from school.** (NEGATIVE—A bully would love to think he or she upset you so much you had to miss school! Plus, it means you are missing important things you should be learning. That's not fair to you.)

Recommended Reading

WHY: To underscore that your child may need to run and get help

READ: *Bullies Are a Pain in the Brain* by Trevor Romain

In this book, the character Trevor Romain says, "You might look a bit foolish running down the street like a maniac but you will look alive!" Help your child understand that it is never a defeat to run. In fact, in some situations it may be the smartest choice.

In fact, there are many techniques that can work. It's also essential to stress that if your son or daughter ever feels in danger, he or she should always run away and get help. Make sure your child realizes, though, that running and getting help go hand in hand. Keeping quiet about a dangerous situation is NEVER a good idea.

Now that you have introduced the idea that there are many ways of reacting to bullies that can be successful, your child is ready to learn the Top Ten Strategies for Handling Bullies, below.

Top Ten Strategies for Handling Bullies

Tested and true, the Top Ten Strategies for Handling Bullies are simple and effective ways of handling bullying situations. These strategies help while the bullying is actually happening and until your child can get to a safe place and obtain help from an adult.

Read and discuss each strategy included on the list below. The strategies are in no particular order, but each one of them should become familiar and almost second nature to your son or daughter. Explain to your child that no single strategy will always work and that one needs to be prepared to try different strategies, to choose the strategy that best fits the situation.

Reading and discussing the Top Ten Strategies for Handling Bullies with your child isn't enough. You need to help your child remember all ten of them and to be ready to use them when and if the strategies are needed in a bullying situation. Here are some learning techniques that will help your child develop mastery of all ten strategies.

- **Practice.** Role-playing works well: Take turns being the bully. Before you ask him or her to role-play, remind your child to be conscious of treating people with respect. This activity should be fun. Cruel personal statements or comments (even in the context of the role-playing) are not acceptable. Keep the comments general. Like learning to throw a ball, the more your child practices the better he or she will get.

- **Summarize.** Have your child tell you all ten of the strategies in his or her own words. This is something you can do when you're traveling in the car, doing chores together, talking just before bedtime, or sharing a few moments of uninterrupted time.

- **Reread.** Ask your son or daughter to record the strategies in a little booklet or notepad, small enough to tuck in his or her pants pocket and easily located for ready reference and reviewing.

- **Illustrate.** Tell your child to get out the markers and create a big poster for his or her room or other easy-to-see location—where the strategies can be read and reread every day. For this art activity, you may find the abbreviated list on page 69 a helpful resource.

It is always appropriate to invent other strategies that could be used in a bullying situation. Certainly, there are more than ten strategies that can help your child. As you consider what strategies mesh well with your child's personality and particular bullying situation, make every effort to include your child's practical ideas. Add those strategies to the list!

STRATEGY #1: SAY "SO?"

When a bully confronts your child with put-downs, this is a great way to respond. The simple reaction "So?" does the job. The encounter gets boring, really boring, for a bully who gets the same response each time he or she says something mean or hurtful. Draw attention to the fact that the action is small, but effective. After hearing "So?" several times, the bully will walk away . . . and perhaps continue to hurl insults over his or her shoulder. But the bully will walk away.

Recommended Reading

WHY: To highlight that simple actions can be powerful strategies

READ: *The Meanest Thing to Say* by Bill Cosby

In this story, Little Bill, a character your child may recognize from television, meets a new boy named Michael. Michael challenges him to play a game called the "Twelve Meanest Things to Say to Somebody." This makes Little Bill uncomfortable and he doesn't know what to do. He tells his dad, who gives him a simple, one-word strategy—"So?" The strategy works. Every time Michael says something mean, Little Bill replies, "So?" Michael soon becomes tired of the game.

If possible, introduce the "So?" strategy by first sharing *The Meanest Thing to Say* with your child. If you don't have a copy of the book, use the summary above to retell the story in your own words. You could personalize it by putting yourself in as the Little Bill character (don't use the names of real bullies or bullied children, as it puts them in an awkward position), or make up a whole new story that illustrates the same idea.

STRATEGY #2: BE A BROKEN RECORD!

This strategy is closely related to "So?" except that the bullied child chooses a statement to calmly repeat over and over until the bully walks away.

A child might repeat statements such as "I don't deserve to be treated this way" or "Stop talking to me like that." Here's what an exchange might resemble:

BULLY: *Oh, look at your hair! Did someone cut it with a lawnmower?*

YOUR CHILD: *Stop talking to me like that.*

BULLY: *Oh, I'm scared. What are you gonna do?*

YOUR CHILD: *Stop talking to me like that.*

BULLY: *What's wrong with you? Cat got your tongue?*

YOUR CHILD: *Stop talking to me like that.*

BULLY: *"Stop talking to me like that!"* (mimicking)

YOUR CHILD: *Stop talking to me like that.*

Bully snorts and walks off.

STRATEGY #3: STAND TALL!

Point out to your child that one's body language and voice volume make a difference in how others see us. Demonstrate what you mean by acting out different reactions to a bully's ceaseless teasing. Explain that defending oneself often means standing tall or behaving in a manner that commands respect. A confrontation with a bully is no time to worry about being polite.

A demonstration might look like this: Hunch over and walk around looking at the ground. Then, use a whispery voice to say: "Oh, please don't do that to me. C'mon, please stop it. I don't like that. You're hurting me!"

When you've finished your demonstration, have your child practice doing the opposite: look right at you and use a loud voice to say in clear terms what he or she wants the bully to do. Afterwards, brainstorm a list of short, direct statements your son or daughter could make. Keep the list for future reference and practice.

STRATEGY #4: BREATHE DEEP!

When we are feeling scared, nervous, or angry, our body's first response is to tense up. Have your child show you how he or she looks when scared, then angry. (You might invite your child to notice how muscles clench, fists ball up, and faces grimace when we are feeling angry.) When our bodies are tense, our brains have to work harder to think clearly. In stressful situations, learning some basic relaxation skills can help us stay calm and make positive decisions about what to do. Here is an exercise your child can do to clear his or her mind:

1. Take a deep breath through the nose and hold it for a count of four. Then blow it quietly out through the mouth. As he or she blows out slowly, your child should imagine that he or she is blowing all of the tenseness out and away.

2. Breathe deeply two or three more times.

3. Think about what he or she is feeling. Reflect on which bully-proofing strategy to try first.

4. Breathe deeply again.

5. Take action.

Let your son or daughter know that with practice deep breathing becomes an easy, automatic thing to do. Explain that in some bullying situations, your child may feel that there isn't time to do all five steps, and that's okay. Even just breathing deeply once or twice will help your child stay calm and consider what course of action to take.

I model deep breathing for children in my classroom when stressful situations arise—big exams, concert performances, or times when everyone is wound up and things are getting out of hand. It works!

STRATEGY #5: HA, HA, HA! (USE HUMOR.)

The aim of using humor is not to laugh at the bully, but to make a funny comment or joke that defuses the situation. This is a tricky strategy that takes some practice. Here's what I mean by using humor successfully, in ways that stop the bullying without making use of the bully's tactics:

A bully taunts a boy about his new haircut.

BULLY: *Nice haircut, buzzhead!*

NEGATIVE RESPONSES: *Oh, yeah? Where'd you get your haircut, at Lawnmowers' R' Us?* or *Well, at least mine doesn't look like a rat's nest!*

POSITIVE RESPONSES: *Yeah, it's pretty distinctive and special, just like me!* or *Yeah. Makes me look like Einstein, don't you think?* or *It does kind of look like I put my finger in a light socket, doesn't it?*

Sometimes, if a child is comfortable with this strategy, he or she can make gentle jokes about himself or herself (self-deprecating humor). For younger children especially, it's helpful to talk about what makes a comment funny rather than unkind. You might also look at the ways a fictional character like Molly Lou Melon uses humor when dealing with Ronald Durkin. (You'll find more information about this recommended book on page 59.)

STRATEGY #6: USE THE EYES IN THE BACK OF YOUR HEAD!

Children need to be aware of what is going on around them. They need to be watching, listening to, and thinking about what is happening. If they see a bully approaching, they should try to avoid the situation by moving to an area where there are other people. Sometimes, if children knowingly put themselves in a vulnerable situation (e.g., by being alone while reading books), they can circumvent problems by being proactive, by periodically observing their social environment.

To help your child practice this strategy, try this version of the game Stop, Look, and Listen. It is an activity that you can do when you're at a public playground or other venue (such as the beach). To begin, explain that a few times in row you will use an agreed-upon signal (e.g., a whistled tune that only your child will recognize). When your child hears the signal, he or she freezes and looks around the setting. Is your child in close proximity to others? Is he or she alone (and vulnerable to being singled out)? Is there a sibling, friend, or group activity close by that he or she could join in?

STRATEGY #7: SLIP-SLIDE AWAY!

Walking away from a bullying situation prevents a child from being "hooked" into talking to the bully. The Slip-Slide Away strategy entails your child simply turning and walking away from his or her tormentor. This strategy can be used in combination with the Say "So?" or Be a Broken Record! strategy. When dealing with just one bully, this strategy can save your child from having to come up with anything to say. Your son or daughter can just walk away.

Sometimes it isn't as simple as taking a step and just walking away. A bully who is especially eager for engagement may move in front of your child. In that instance, your child should just pivot and walk quickly away in another direction (toward people). And what if the bully follows again? Advise your child to continue walking and turning unexpectedly until either the bully gives up or your child has managed to move to a safer, more populated area.

This strategy is fun to practice when you are at the park. You can turn it into a game. To begin, decide on the "safe spot" you are aiming for. Take turns playing the bully while the other person practices slip-slidin' away! Remember, the goal is to keep moving unexpectedly and repeatedly until you are in a safer spot.

Recommended Reading

WHY: To introduce the strategy of positive self-talk

READ: *The Little Engine That Could* by Watty Piper

Sharing this beloved book and discussing the theme of "I think I can, I think I can . . ." would be an engaging and fitting introduction to the Be a Cheerleader! strategy.

STRATEGY #8: BE A CHEERLEADER!

Children who bully try to make other children feel bad about themselves. Children often listen to what bullies say and often believe their put-downs and criticisms. To some degree, we all listen to the negative things people say about us. How many negative comments do you remember from your teachers, parents, and friends as opposed to all of the positive comments you've received?

You can help your child become his or her own cheerleader. To begin, model how to be your own cheerleader. Ask your child to tease you by declaring that your shoes are ugly. Explain that to react like a cheerleader, you would say positive things to yourself (positive self-talk). You'll need to share your thoughts with your child for this demonstration, but you should clarify that in real life your child should speak to himself or herself silently.

Your positive self-talk might sound like this: "Wow, is that bully wrong. I don't deserve to be talked to that way. I am a great person. I am kind. I would never treat anyone else so badly. I don't need to put anyone down because I like who I am. And . . . I like these shoes. That bully is just plain WRONG!"

Or, you could have your son or daughter create a personal cheer. This cheer would serve as a sort of a chant, rap, or mantra that your child can use anytime a bully begins saying nasty things: "I am kind. I am strong. I am a good person. I LIKE ME!" Ideally, the cheer is catchy so that it's easy to recall in moments of crisis, without even having to think about it.

Positive self-talk is an effective and excellent strategy for children to use (and not only in bullying situations). While it may seem a little artificial, having children repeat their strengths over and over contributes to strengthening self-confidence.

STRATEGY #9: GET HELP!

This is a strategy that goes hand in hand with every other strategy you discuss with your son or daughter. Your child needs to know that he or she can get help—that other people can be supportive.

This is an ideal time to talk to children about the difference between telling and tattling. Barbara Coloroso defines the difference nicely:

> TATTLING: If it will only get another person into trouble, don't
>   tell me.
> TELLING: If it will get you or another child out of trouble, tell me.
> If it is both, I need to know.

Use this response daily. Younger children often "tell" on others, and your response should clearly define whether or not they are telling or tattling.

Once your child understands clearly when it's appropriate to get help, work together to create a list of trustworthy people to whom your child can turn. Whom can your child call, e-mail, or contact with ease? Make sure that your child thinks through with you about who would be most helpful in a bullying situation. (An older sibling's best friend is probably not a good choice.) At the top of the list, write your name, your child's teacher's name, and the names of familiar neighbors. You may want to include school support staff (by name) and trustworthy people in the child's community (for example, a coach). Once the list is complete, encourage your child to post it where he or she can access it easily. As well, you should let people know that they are on your list and to be ready if approached by your child.

STRATEGY #10: BEFRIEND THE BULLY!

At times, being friendly to a bully can make a difference. However, even if a full-fledged friendship doesn't develop, by extending a friendly gesture, a child may make it harder for a bully to target the child who is being kind to

Top Ten Strategies
for Handling Bullies

1   SAY "SO?"

2   BE A BROKEN RECORD!

3   STAND TALL!

4   BREATHE DEEP!

5   HA, HA, HA! (USE HUMOR.)

6   USE THE EYES IN THE BACK OF YOUR HEAD!

7   SLIP-SLIDE AWAY!

8   BE A CHEERLEADER!

9   GET HELP!

10   BEFRIEND THE BULLY!

him or her. Kind overtures of friendship might include: saying hello, showing receptive facial expressions or body language (e.g., a smile), inviting him or her to join a game or activity, or anything that lets the bully know that the past can stay in the past.

If your child decides to take up this strategy, it's important for him or her to have a sense that the bully is somewhat approachable. Many bullies are not approachable at all! Help your child to understand that, as with everything else, there are no guarantees—the bully may remain a bully. (To learn more about friendship building in general, turn to Chapter Five.)

 Recommended Reading

WHY: To show that sometimes kindness deflates a bully's aggression

READ: *Bully* by Judith Caseley

Mickey is harassed by Jack, a boy who steals Mickey's cookies, breaks his pencil, and is generally mean—especially since Jack's new baby brother arrived. Mickey's dad listens and provides ideas on how to stand up to Jack, but Mickey is so intimidated he doesn't try them. His mother suggests that Mickey "Love thine enemy." His sister agrees, telling him to take extra cookies for Jack . . . a first step toward making Jack a friend. Mickey's best strategy turns out to be "make him laugh," a strategy that ultimately helps turn Jack into a buddy.

Creating Your Child's Personal Bully-Proofing Plan

Now that these strategies have been introduced, it makes sense for your child to follow in your footsteps and create his or her own plan for what to do if bullied. This personal plan is related to the plan you have created, but is less complicated.

In preparation, you'll need:

♦ A copy of your Parental Plan of Action (to use as a springboard)

_____'s Action Plan

If I'm being bullied, first I will

_____

_____

_____

And then I will tell _____ .

If that doesn't work, then I will try

_____

_____

_____

And then I will tell _____ .

My emergency strategy will be

_____

_____

_____

And I will get help by telling _____ .

If I ever feel that I am in danger, I will run and tell an adult

RIGHT AWAY!

♦ A copy of the fill-in plan provided on page 71 (If your child prefers to copy the language onto another sheet of paper, that's fine, too.)

♦ The poster your child made to illustrate the Top Ten Strategies for Handling Bullies (See page 69 for reference.)

♦ The reference list of trustworthy people your child made to support his or her Get Help! strategy (page 68)

To begin, discuss your Parental Plan of Action. Talk about the steps you went through and how it helps you feel in control because you know what you plan to do if your child has a bullying problem. Remind your child that, as with all plans, he or she will need to be flexible. A situation may arise where following a set plan no longer makes sense. Generally, though, a plan of action helps people take key steps toward solving a problem.

Ask your child to choose two strategies (from the Top Ten Strategies for Handling Bullies list) with which he or she feels most comfortable. Then give your child a copy of the fill-in plan to write on. Explain that to complete the plan, he or she needs to decide on an "emergency" strategy as well. This is any strategy a student is willing to try as a last resort. While your child is creating a plan, support the work but don't do it for him or her.

Your child needs to feel ownership of his or her plan. For a younger child, act as a scribe. You can record his or her ideas, while your son or daughter adds illustrations or decorations. To add a level of formality to the plan, attach gold-tone seals or stickers (available in office supply stores) and/or a ribbon to a corner. When the plan is complete, tell your child to sign the bottom and date it. Then you sign the plan as well. The last step involves showing it off to siblings, friends, grandparents, and teachers. Celebrate its completion! If your child is excited and enthusiastic about the plan, he or she is more likely to put it into action.

Rallying School Support

Now, with plans in place, you and your child are in a position to deal with bullies if and when they become a problem. These two plans will prove especially helpful if you need your child's school to become involved.

While it's always a good idea to have regular, positive contact with your child's teacher and principal, it becomes essential when expecting their help with bullying. Meet with your child's teacher. Explain what the problem is and the plan your child has created. Give the teacher a copy of the plan (and your Parental Plan of Action, if you are comfortable with that) so that they are aware of how you are dealing with it at home.

Ask about your school's bully-proofing program and make sure it fits with your aims and philosophy. If not, it may be worth becoming involved with your parent-teacher organization to help create a community-supported, whole-school plan. To help guide you through the process, you might read *Creating a Bully-Free Classroom* (McMullen, 2005). In it, I've provided ideas for bully-proofing your child's school.

By now, your child has a clear understanding of bullying (and what it is), knows that he or she is not alone, realizes that many people have the same experiences and fears, and feels knowledgeable that many things can be done about it. Your child has a toolbox of strategies to use and, best of all, a plan of action.

All of these things give your child something that bullies back away from: confidence and strength to stand up and face a tormentor. Empowered children are tough to bully.

Development, it turns out, occurs through this process of progressively more complex exchange between a child and somebody else— especially somebody who's crazy about that child.

~Urie Bronfenbrenner, psychologist

 **CHAPTER FOUR**

What If the Bully Is My Child?

The focus on bullying tends to be on bullied children and how to help them, but what do you do if your child is the bully? It's a scenario that no parent wants to encounter. But it's a reality— someone harasses bullied children. That someone may be your child.

After realizing that your child is a bully, your immediate response may be to feel guilty and overwhelmed. You're being faced with the reality of your child's behavior. Like many parents, you may feel the need to be given concrete, repeated evidence that your child is bullying others before you will accept that your child needs help.

While it is necessary for you to reflect upon the reasons your child is

> "[Bullying is] . . . a great strategy for getting what you want [immediately]. You push the little girl off of the tricycle; you get the tricycle. A lot of aggressive kids think aggression works. They think about one outcome, but not about the others."
> Gary W. Ladd, professor of psychology, Arizona State University (in *Why Doesn't Anybody Like Me? A Guide to Raising Socially Confident Kids*, Marano, 1998)

RESEARCH IN THE

Bullies Grow to Be Adults

As adults many bullies end up being hampered by their aggression. Some end up in trouble with the law and experience difficulties in adult relationships (in marriages or at work). In fact, studies consistently reveal that most bullies go into a "downward spiral" throughout life, their behavior interfering with learning, friendships, jobs, intimate relationships, income, and mental health. (Marano, page 132)

involved in bullying behavior, it is not the case that your child is "bad" and little can be done. Bullies need to be held accountable for their behavior. They need to work on social skills by being presented with new ways of interacting with others. Parents and others need to work on helping these children deal with their aggressive behavior patterns. Not only is this possible, it's essential for you to be a positive force for change with your child.

Some Reasons Children Bully

Among the many reasons children bully is family dynamics. Studies have shown that family dynamics play a large part in forming aggressive behavior (see page 19, Chapter One). But there are shared factors and traits.

Bullies usually begin exhibiting aggressive behaviors while young. In fact, you can often recognize bullies even during their preschool years. By the time they enter high school, they have earned a reputation for aggression.

Aggressive children tend to have a negative view of the world, feeling that aggression is the best way to get what they want. They believe that the world is an unfriendly place and think that "getting back" at someone and dominating and/or controlling people are the best ways to deal with others. They have not learned to be flexible, nor have they developed the resources necessary to help them interpret other people's behavior. Bullies often see other people's actions in black and white terms, unable to interpret the intent behind someone's actions. Empathy toward others is not something these children are able to achieve.

Another common feature of aggressive children is an inability to see the real social outcomes of their own behavior. That is, they may believe they are popular and other children like them, when the opposite is often true. Bullies have trouble accepting responsibility for their behavior, blam-

RESEARCH
IN THE

Bullies With Friends

It turns out bullies form friendships without much difficulty. Research suggests that children who are friends with bullies may share positive attitudes toward aggression and participate in the bullying, too. (Nansel et al, 2001)

ing everyone but themselves for problems they encounter.

Dr. Dan Olweus defines bullies this way: Bullying involves *aggressive* behavior with *negative intent* directed from one child to another where there is a *power difference*. The behavior is repeated over time and becomes *chronic* (Marano, 1998).

While they may not target the same child repeatedly, these children have repeated bullying episodes with many people. To help bullies most effectively, it's essential to set aside stereotypes and focus on behaviors they have in common.

Children who bully may:

♦ exhibit aggressive behavior (even as a young child)

♦ believe aggression is an acceptable way to resolve conflicts

♦ show aggression as part of a general rule-breaking stance

♦ abuse others physically or verbally

♦ have a need to dominate others

♦ manipulate the relationships of others (to be mean)

♦ get into fights (and blame others for starting them)

♦ be quick to interpret accidents and other neutral events as deliberate acts of hostility

♦ lack an understanding of pain in others

♦ feel no anxiety

♦ feel no loneliness

♦ have two or three friends who are also aggressive

♦ hang out with increasingly younger children

♦ believe they are well liked by other children (in general)

(*Adapted from* Why Doesn't Anybody Like Me? *Marano, 1998.*)

Why Is *My* Child Bullying Others?

While there are many factors that can influence your child's behavior, only you can evaluate and make adjustments to circumstances at home that may be contributing to bullying behavior. Looking at the behavior patterns of your child and coming up with a plan to change his or her behavior must include a look at your child's home experiences. Perhaps your child is:

- ◆ observing difficulties between parents (separation, divorce, remarriage)

- ◆ adjusting to a new family situation (single parent, new sibling, a move to a new community, death of a family member or pet)

- ◆ spending less time with a parent (who may work long hours)

- ◆ undergoing a loosening of family ties (a family member relocated far away)

- ◆ encountering an emphasis on technology and less on face-to-face social interaction

- ◆ experiencing the influence of violent television shows and video games

- ◆ finding less time to be a kid

We often don't realize the power of our words and actions as parents. For instance, how do you relate to strangers? What about people within and around your family? Whether we like it or not, our children are always watching, listening, and imitating our behaviors, speech, and beliefs. Your child looks up to you. You are the most important role model your child will ever have. And you may be inadvertently sending messages that support your child's bullying behaviors.

It's difficult to face ourselves in the mirror and really look at what role we are playing in problems that arise. However, for your child to make any meaningful changes, it is essential to develop an understanding and acceptance of your family dynamics and how they may be coloring the situation. You cannot change what you don't acknowledge, and it's unfair to expect your child to change if you do not work on the issues that may be affecting him or her. Begin by asking yourself some questions (see page 78).

Children Mirror What They See

Modeling is one aspect of being a parent that we often forget about in the bustle of daily life, but it is one of the most important things you do for your child. Your child is constantly observing and absorbing what he or she sees and hears you do, which can be quite overwhelming if you stop to think about it.

When you are interacting with your child or with other adults or

Some Questions to Ask Yourself

♦ Do you actively initiate conversations with your child about important things going on in his or her life? Do you listen and offer positive feedback?

♦ Do you spend unstructured time together that gives your child the time and space to open up and talk about himself or herself?

♦ Do you model empathetic behavior for your child?

♦ Do you model aggressive behavior toward another family member?

♦ Would some people view you as confrontational?

♦ Do you encourage your child to stand up for himself or herself by hitting back or being aggressive?

♦ How do you tend to react when someone talks to you about your child's behavior?

♦ In front of your child, are you critical of your child's school or teachers?

♦ Do you feel that the school should deal with behavior issues such as bullying or other inappropriate behaviors without involving you?

♦ Do you feel comfortable with the discipline techniques you use? In what ways are they effective or ineffective?

(*Adapted from* Questions for Parents, *Liz Carnell, and* Bullying UK, 1999–2007. www.bullying.co.uk)

RESEARCH IN THE

Neurotransmitters and Aggressive Behavior

In an effort to learn more about aggression, some scientists look at smaller animals and the role of neurotransmitters in the brain. "In golden hamsters, offensive aggression is facilitated by vasopressin and inhibited by serotonin." A series of experiments conducted by Yvon Delville (1998) and his colleagues at the University of Massachusetts Medical Center, Worcester, Massachusetts, ". . . tested whether these neurotransmitter systems respond to modifications resulting from the stress of threat and attack (i.e., social subjugation) during puberty."

In his article in American Scientist about Delville's experiments, author Michael Szpir comments that "No one believes that there is a simple relation between the brain's biochemistry and the behavior of an animal—be it a hamster or a human being—but studies such as Delville's do make one wonder about the disposition of neurotransmitters in the brains of all the angry young men in the schoolyards."

children, your child is learning lessons related to having successful (or unsuccessful) relationships with others. If you set aside time and make your child feel valued and your child knows that what he or she has to say is important, your child will tend to value what others have to say. If you model respectful and assertive (but not aggressive) behavior when dealing with a conflict situation, your child will see that, too. If you tend to be critical of others, overreact, act aggressively, or are negative or dismissive of others' views and feelings, your child will follow suit.

None of us is perfect. We all lose our cool (and our perspective) once in a while. However, when we as adults act poorly, we must make sure that our children understand that we realize we have behaved badly and will accept the consequences of that behavior by apologizing or making reparation in some way. Parents who are unaware, unapologetic, or unconcerned about the results of aggression are sending a strong message to their children. There are even those who believe that bullying is a normal part of growing up—parents who do not realize that bullying damages the bullied child *and* the bully himself.

Many bullies tend to be argumentative generally. They break the rules and in most situations are defiant and aggressive. Additionally, many bullies have a difficult time accepting responsibility for their actions. As you begin to think about the ways in which you use discipline in your family, consider your answers to the questions that follow:

> **Assertive behavior:** Having the confidence to speak up and stand up for yourself when you are unhappy or disagree with someone. You are able to defend your viewpoint and possibly work out a mutual solution to the problem.
>
> **Aggressive behavior:** Using threats, force, or even violence to deal with a conflict or disagreement.

- ◆ How do you hold your child accountable for his or her behavior?

- ◆ Are you *consistently* applying consequences and following through on them?

- ◆ Is your child able to negotiate or "talk you down" by shifting the blame to others?

- ◆ Do you feel after disciplining your child that he or she really doesn't "get it" and hasn't learned from the experience?

- ◆ Is your child inadvertently being rewarded for aggressive behavior? (For example, does a suspension mean your child gets to spend some one-on-one time with you or another supportive adult?)

COMPETITION AND AGGRESSION Sometimes our best efforts to be the cheering section for our children ends up sending the message that aggression in life equals respect and love. Aggression in children, especially boys, is something that many parents, men in particular, expect to see, whether

---

Fans or Fanatics?

Think about some of the adults you've seen at youth games and sport competitions. In what ways are those adults supporting children who are learning to grapple with an array of volatile emotions? In what ways are they advocating aggression? Assertiveness?

In his book, *The Challenging Child*, Dr. Stanley Greenspan explains that in some settings, feelings of "rage and competition . . . [can] overload children. But against a background of warmth, love, empathy, and acceptance, there is nothing like a little bit of anger or jealousy to get the motor going!" (Greenspan, 1995)

on the sports field or in another competitive setting. Competition is a reality. But focusing only on the winning and not paying attention to the other aspects of the competition, namely bettering one's own performance rather than achieving something at the expense of others, is unhealthy. For example, playing hockey can be a pressure cooker for young men—with some parents urging their child to not "play like a wimp," to behave aggressively, to go for the puck and become the star of the game. Conversely, most coaches of youth teams find that emphasizing personal skill-building, teamwork, and a sense of fair play makes for not only a stronger team but also happier, emotionally healthier individuals.

Getting Your Child Back on Track

Bullies are victims of their own behavior. The reality is that they isolate themselves from others, and from ultimately feeling successful in life, because they lack two things: social skills and an ability to regulate their own destructive behavior (Marano, 1998).

The question then becomes, what can you do to move your child off this path? If your child is showing bullying tendencies when young, that is the time to get help and try some new strategies that will make a difference.

As all bullies (regardless of chronological age) need to develop stronger, more successful social skills and self-discipline, these are the logical areas to work on with your child.

♦ **Teach your child how to handle frustration** in acceptable, non-aggressive ways. Children need to be exposed to situations where they may encounter frustration or failure, and they need specific guidance as to how to properly handle those angry feelings. For example, many parents find that playing board games (a fun activity that brings families together) also offers valuable opportunities to model acceptable behaviors (especially when losing); after all, only one person can win!

♦ **Make sure aggressive behaviors are recognized as such.** Ensure that your child is held accountable for his or her behavior and use consequences fairly and consistently.

◆ **Teach your child better ways of handling anger.** These may include stress-reduction techniques and finding other outlets (e.g., taking anger out on inanimate objects, such as pillows or balls).

◆ **Model non-aggressive behaviors for your child.** Aggressive, hostile behavior is never an appropriate way to solve a problem and it usually leads to bigger complications. If this is happening in your household, you need to learn more appropriate social skills and self-discipline techniques for yourself or other family members, and put them into practice. Get help! Remember, your behavior or your spouse's may indeed be part of the problem and getting help will be a huge step toward improving both your life and your child's.

◆ **Teach your child conflict resolution skills.** (These skills are discussed in detail in Chapter Six.) By giving children another option for solving problems with others, you reduce the need for violence. Children who like the power and lack empathy for others gain from this approach as well. By learning that they will be held accountable for their behavior and hearing firsthand how they have hurt someone else, the reality and consequences of their behavior choices become clearer to them.

◆ **Shake up your interaction with your child.** Think about how you usually interact with your son or daughter. Do you half-listen as you try to do other things, frown a lot, talk only about their poor behaviors or talk superficially about their interests? Look at your child as he or she speaks, really listen to what he or she says, nod, smile, and give positive cues (especially when you notice positive, non-aggressive behavior). In other words, try to focus on your child in a positive way more often. Ask questions about what is going on in your child's life. A child who feels that you value him or her and that you notice the good things that he or she does will be happier and more receptive to what you have to say.

For more information about teaching your child social skills, turn to Chapter Five. You can also check your local library for the many excellent parenting books available. Or you might ask your child's teachers for their recommendations.

Child Development and Empathy

How old does a child need to be to understand what other people are feeling? Our experience with empathy begins when we see how our parents respond to our cries when we're infants. As toddlers, developing empathy shows itself in skills such as sharing and taking turns. Dr. Lawrence Kutner, a nationally known clinical psychologist, explains that the development of empathy is tied to the development of certain cognitive, social, and emotional skills.

> *"When a child is about 5, he can learn about empathy by talking about hypothetical problems. How would you feel if someone took a toy away from you? . . . By the time a child is 8, he can grapple with more complex moral decisions in which he must realize someone else's feelings may be different from his own."*

(*Adapted from* How Children Develop Empathy, *Lawrence Kutner, October 2007. www.drkutner.com*)

 ## Recommended Reading

There are many parenting books out there that offer great advice. One author that I highly recommend is Barbara Coloroso. Her books include:

Kids Are Worth It: Giving Your Kids the Gift of Inner Discipline

Parenting With Wit and Wisdom in Times of Chaos and Loss

Winning at Parenting Without Beating Your Kids!

Who's in Charge Anyway? How Parents Can Teach Children to Do the Right Thing

Parenting Through Crisis: Helping Kids in Times of Loss, Grief and Change

The Bully, the Bullied, and the Bystander: From Pre-School to High School–How Parents and Teachers Can Help Break the Cycle of Violence

These books are readily available. For more information visit Coloroso's Web site, www.kidsareworthit.com.

Finding a Positive Groove

Children who bully rarely have the chance to have people respond to them in a positive way. They tend to fall into a negative behavior pattern early because their relationships with others, particularly adults, tend to be negative ones. In effect, they may continue to bully as a kind of self-fulfilling prophecy. "Well, if they already think I'm going to bully someone, then I guess I probably will." They may never have experienced the feeling that their actions resulted in a positive result for someone else. Bullies need to see how good it feels to help other people, and experience the reality of the adage "Do unto others as you would have them do unto you."

A bully needs to see that his or her behavior has a negative result and that positive behavior has a positive payback. When you see kindness in action, you should respond immediately. My favorite way of recognizing appropriate behavior is to create a note on the computer and make a few photocopies. Or, you could buy special note cards that you use just for the occasion of saying "I caught you . . . doing something terrific, that is!" Often we keep a close eye on our children to spot misbehaviors. Yet, catching constructive behavior has an amazing impact.

Writing a quick note is an effective (and unusual) way to communicate with your child. Be sure to specifically state and reinforce what you saw. To write, "You were being a good friend" isn't descriptive enough. Instead, try to name the behavior: "You were taking turns with Latisha." Put the note somewhere and let your child discover it privately. You might leave the note on your child's pillow, tucked into a lunchbox, or (my favorite) hidden in a shoe. Leaving notes is a kind of encouragement that is always a hit. Children value the concreteness of it; having something in writing is real proof that they did something well. Plus, a child can keep the note and read it again and again.

I use some of the following techniques in my classroom, where one of

> Dear Michael,
>
> I am so proud of you! I saw you sharing your Popsicle with your cousin, without even being asked. You made Devin so happy!
>
> Way to go!
>
> Love, Mom

the toughest children I worked with pretended to scrunch up his positive note from me up and throw it away, but when no one was looking, carefully retrieved it, flattened it out, and kept it taped to the inside of his pencil box for the rest of the year.

Every time a child feels good about behavior, it's another step in building a positive view of himself or herself. Here are some more ways to acknowledge and encourage your child:

♦ **Use nonverbal signals**, especially in public situations not conducive to more showy recognition. A wink or a thumbs-up is an effective way to say, "I caught you doing something good!"

♦ **Have your child volunteer with you at a community event.** Get him or her involved in helping others (with supervision) and relating to others in a positive way. Often, the other people who are participating turn out to be excellent role models.

♦ **Ask your child to teach others.** This method helps some children really blossom. Your child's teacher may be able to arrange for your child to work with a younger child daily for a short period of time on a specific need. For example, your child could work on reading or basic math facts with a younger "study buddy" for ten minutes a day. I have seen many students who were difficult in my classroom settle down and become responsible, enthusiastic "teachers" of younger children.

In Action: Manuel

Manuel caused upheaval in my classroom whenever he could. Then, when he became a "study buddy" to a kindergarten child who needed help learning colors, Manuel became enthusiastic. In fact, he developed lessons at home that he could share with this buddy. His excitement when his student learned the colors was something to see! Manuel helped a few other students and always earned glowing comments and praise from the students and teachers involved. While he still had many problems, Manuel felt successful and became more cooperative and pleasant to be around. Manuel had learned how to positively channel his need to be noticed and accepted by others.

RESEARCH

IN THE

Inclined to Feel Empathy

A recent study at the University of Chicago used functional Magnetic Resonance Imaging (fMRI) scans to see how children's brains process feelings of empathy. In the study, researchers worked with typical children, ages 7 to 12.

Jean Decety, Professor in the Departments of Psychology and Psychiatry, says the findings suggest that children process empathy in much the same way adults do. Children appear to be "hard-wired" to feel empathy for others in pain and are ". . . not entirely the product of parental guidance or other nurturing." Researchers hope their insights into how the normal brain processes empathy can shed light on how ". . . brain impairments influence anti-social behavior, such as bullying."

(Adapted from Brain Scans Demonstrate a Child's Empathy, *Rick Nauert, July 2008. http://psychcentral.com)*

The Role of Empathy

Developing empathy is a key part of the puzzle in helping bullies to recognize and care about the impact their behaviors have on others. You can foster its development by routinely asking your child these three questions and using the techniques that follow:

1. How is that person feeling?

2. How can you tell how he or she is feeling?

3. How would you feel if that happened to you?

Model an awareness of how others may be feeling and your reactions to their emotions. Talk about why you think someone acted in a certain way, whether it's on a television show or in real life. Here are some examples:

"I bet Mark felt really angry when he saw Yoko using his Lego without asking, and that's why he yelled at her."

"Mrs. Lewis looked really tired today when I picked you up from school. I wonder if all of her extra work in planning the holiday concert is getting to her. Maybe I'll phone her and offer some help."

"Poor Mr. Rogers across the street. He broke his leg skiing. I bet he's feeling sad, and I know a broken leg must hurt. I think I'll make him some brownies. Want to help?"

Talk with your child about people and their reactions to aggression. (Again, books and television programs are helpful.) Use the three empathy questions each time. While you may not enjoy sounding like a broken record, using those same three questions helps your child remember them easily. When he or she remembers them, your child will likely begin asking those same questions habitually. That's your goal!

Help your child become more effective at reading the body language, tone of voice, and nonverbal communication of others. Billboards, magazine pictures, ads, and other pictures give your child a chance to study these cues and think about the feelings behind them.

Empathy is a cornerstone of building and maintaining successful relationships and is discussed in greater detail in Chapter Five.

The Right Kind of Power

Most bullies enjoy the power that they have when they bully another person. Feeling powerful is a big payoff to children who may feel powerless in other areas of their lives. It's important to give your child power and responsibility in a variety of ways to combat his or her tendency to bully others.

Making Decisions

Teaching children to make decisions for themselves is an essential tool, not only for reducing their need to bully others but also because children must have the experience, confidence, and wisdom to make good decisions as they grow older. As Barbara Coloroso discusses in *Kids Are Worth It!* (2002), their decisions don't have to be major ones, and you structure the choices they have. Small children can decide which cereal they will eat by choosing between the two boxes you have put out for them. As they get older, the choices they are given are increased, but are still structured by you. ("From four o'clock until seven, you need to do your homework, put away your laundry, and then have some free time. You need to decide your schedule.")

Of course, your child will also need to learn that not making a good choice has its costs. Don't give in and give them what they want if they don't like the choices—that teaches aggressive children that they don't have to follow the rules and they can always get what they want. They need to learn that there are real-life consequences to their decisions, just as there are for adults.

Taking on Responsibilities

Everyone needs to be needed. Feeling that what you do is important and makes a difference to your family is a great boost to a child's self-esteem. Even young children can do basic chores. One family I know expected their son, age 9, to set the table for dinner. When he resisted (or forgot!), they all sat at an empty table, waiting . . . and waiting. He realized quickly that doing his job meant that his family would have dinner and not before. His contribution meant something, and he took his responsibility seriously from then on.

Tackling Setbacks

If you try some or all of these strategies and your child's bullying behaviors continue, it is time to look for professional help. Talk to your family doctor, your minister, or your child's teacher. They can be great resources for accessing help.

Remember, your child is not "bad." On the contrary, your child needs to learn new ways of behaving, and you may need to learn additional strategies for parenting. Though it can be difficult not to become discouraged, take inspiration from the ways in which you've supported your child. Look for support groups that may be helpful for you. You need support as you and your child work through these issues. (You'll find a list of resources on page 146.)

Working With Your Child's School

Finally, involving your child's school is a key factor in dealing with these bullying issues. While it is difficult to hear negative things about your child, it is important for you to maintain clear, consistent, and regular communication with your child's teacher and principal. Daily home journals, weekly phone calls, and other ways of staying in touch with the school really make a difference in how well you feel the school understands and supports your child's concerted efforts.

LEAD THE WAY While some parents feel it should be the school that initiates and maintains contact, the reality is that most teachers are overwhelmed with all they have to do. You may need to take the initiative. Remember, too, that while you should ask for information on your child's negative behaviors, **you must also ask about, and emphasize, the positives that you and your child's teacher observe in all areas.** You all need a balanced view about your child and what he or she is doing.

Make sure that you keep track of meetings with staff members. This paper trail may become essential if you feel the school team is not meeting your child's needs and you need to contact superintendents or others in the system. As you follow your child's progress, bear in mind the limitations that your school works under.

- Staff members can't legally release personal information about other students involved in conflicts.

- A district may not have staff to provide counseling or specialized help for your child.

- Teachers and principals can't be expected to deal with situations that occur off school property, although they should be made aware of any problems.

- Your school may not have a clear bully-proofing policy. You can, however, help your parent-teacher organization set one in place.

Real-Life Consequences

Bullies must experience consequences for their behavior, but those consequences must make sense, be workable, and be fair. Think about consequences you feel would be successful. If a consequence seems unduly harsh, think carefully about an alternate consequence with which you would be comfortable. **Having no consequence, or one with an outcome that carries no impact, is not a solution to a serious problem.**

If bullying occurs in the classroom or school setting, ask that your child be closely supervised, no matter what the activity, and that the behavior or work required meet an acceptable standard. It's not effective to apply a consequence and then accept a shoddy or incomplete effort. The most important thing that you and your child's school must agree upon is that, with any consequence for bullying, the consequence needs to be tailor-made to fit the child. **Children who bully must be treated with respect and never be expected to do an activity that would place them in an embarrassing situation.** Here are some suggestions for consequences you could advocate and that would be workable in a school setting. Your child could:

♦ walk with a supervisor during recess/lunch, who would keep a tally of kind behavior seen by other students

♦ miss recess or another non-core school activity; use that supervised time to write a plan for future behavior

♦ write a contract for future behavior and, along with parents, teacher, and principal, sign it

♦ research and present a short report to the class about people who believed in nonviolence (e.g., Gandhi)

♦ use free time at lunch or after school to create anti-bullying posters

♦ find an age-appropriate book about bullying (fiction or nonfiction), then read it and create a book report to present to the principal or a younger class

♦ make a comprehensive list of the pros and cons of being a bully

♦ design a poster or cartoon that shows five to ten ways of being a friend to someone

♦ create a big book about how to be a friend or how to be kind to others, then share it with a class of younger students

Having your school principal or other significant adult involved in your anti-bullying plan is key. His or her support is invaluable and adds weight to your efforts in the eyes of your child. Most administrators will be pleased to work with you in a positive way and appreciate your support and willingness to work with the school. Remember, too, that principals don't take pleasure in being the "heavy." Most want to work with you, not against you.

How Mentors Can Help

Since bullies often have negative experiences with a particular teacher or school principal, it can be beneficial to switch things around and have children work in a mentorship-style relationship. Likewise, some children who bully (or have behavioral issues) are seen in a negative light. So mentoring is a move that can be a positive experience for everyone. Ongoing, consistent, and positive attention from an adult can have a huge impact on a child's behavior. (And it may help a principal remember why he or she got into this profession in the first place!)

By meeting regularly, consistently, and kindly, the adult can help your child begin to feel that he or she is "a good person" and valued. While the adult or principal takes a lead role in this mentoring relationship, you should be aware of his or her limitations. You, as the parent, may need to help facilitate this mentoring (e.g., providing materials for activities or arranging to pick up your child after school instead of having him or her take the bus). To help foster a positive relationship between a mentor and your child, consider these collaborative activities:

- ◆ eating lunch together outside (while, for example, bird watching)
- ◆ learning a new hobby (e.g., woodworking)
- ◆ doing a jigsaw puzzle
- ◆ experimenting with science (e.g., baking)
- ◆ working the AV equipment, microphone, or computer during assemblies
- ◆ researching a mutual topic of interest

Whatever your child and mentor do, it must be enjoyable for both of them. Each activity must be interactive; watching a video together means they both lose the opportunity to learn about each other. Ideally, it is a special, one-on-one time to talk, laugh, tell jokes, and deepen their relationship. Tutoring a child in a subject area should be kept for another time, unless it is something the child desperately wants to do. The emphasis should be on helping the child feel that he or she is important to someone and that he or she is capable and valued in a non-judgmental atmosphere.

Some people may feel that mentoring is rewarding a bully's behavior in some way. That's not the intent. How will bullies feel valued and be involved in a positive way with others unless they have the opportunities to learn how?

It's important that bullies realize that they will still be held accountable for their behavior and must face the consequences each time they are involved in bullying, even if the principal is their mentor. Of course, dealing with the consequences of your behavior with someone you like, and who you know likes you, may have deeper impact on a child than we realize. Knowing that you've let down someone who believes in you is a humbling experience.

Having a child who is a bully is a fact of life for some parents, but it should not be a cause for desperation or despair. Instead, by looking at your family dynamics, helping your child learn new behavior patterns and new ways of interacting with others, working closely with the school, and getting professional help if you need it, your child can face his or her future with a positive outlook.

Friendship is born at that moment when one person says to another: What! You too? I thought I was the only one.

~C. S. Lewis, English essayist and juvenile novelist

Luck is what happens when preparation meets opportunity.

~Elmer Letterman, broker and author

©Jupiter Images

CHAPTER FIVE

We All Need Friends

Social skills enable us to make and keep healthy relationships with others. Parents are usually concerned about their child's academic and physical development, but may neglect to support the development of social skills. Developing social competence has a huge impact on a child's future. If a child is not socially successful, it will affect his or her job prospects, social status, and, ultimately, self-esteem. It is true that "no man is an island." We all need to know how to get along successfully with others.

Initiating and maintaining successful relationships with peers and adults are important skills that children need to learn and understand. How to make a friend, be a good friend, and handle problems that occur

Sarah sits under a tree on the edge of the playground, watching a group of her classmates playing tag. She looks eagerly at one girl who approaches her but says nothing as she runs by. Sarah is alone this recess.

Diego arrives on Monday morning, new to the school. He is shy, and he looks at the ground when the teacher introduces him to the class. He is partnered up with Sid, who shows him around but is flummoxed by Diego's whispered answers and obvious unhappiness. Sid takes him

between friends are all important social skills that help children accept, empathize with, and respect others. Children who exhibit these skills have a huge advantage—being comfortable making and keeping friends has an enormous impact on a child's self-image as a capable, likeable person.

In *How Kids Make Friends* (1995) author Lonnie Michelle remarks:

> *Kids who are skilled at making friends have many advantages over most children. The ability to make friends helps a child build a healthy self-esteem at an early age. Children who make friends easily tend to be happier and feel better about themselves. If your child is fortunate enough to learn these skills when they are young, there is a strong likelihood that he or she will . . . have healthy self-esteem throughout life.*

In particular, children who bully seem to lack an understanding of how friendship works. Therefore, the main goal of any discussion about getting along with other people must be to develop tolerance, respect, and empathy for others. As well, all children need opportunities to discuss, observe, and practice these skills. Learning how to interact in a positive way is something that bullied children and bullies alike must learn. Like all other skills, these need to be taught and practiced. You may

The Too-Quiet Child

You can help a child by trying to look through his or her eyes. To that end, here are some observations about the "too quiet" child, who may . . .

- tend to fall through the cracks (in the family or classroom setting) because he or she makes so little noise
- barely tune in during group activities, and stay uninvolved
- get caught up in a cycle—lack of participation makes him or her unsure of how to participate, even when he or she is willing to try
- benefit from friendly overtures from peers and adults (e.g., smiles)

Adapted from Fresh Approaches to Working With Problematic Behavior *by Adele M. Brodkin (Scholastic, 2001)*

Matthew storms in the front door, slamming it hard. "I hate Joey. He's supposed to be my best friend in the world but now he's friends with that new kid." He hurls himself down on the couch, and picks up the

expect children to naturally know these things, especially if you yourself have always been outgoing. In reality, many children need explicit instructions about developing and maintaining friendships.

Social Skills 101

What are the important social skills for children to learn? Psychologists Barbara and Gregory Markway (2005) highlight these:

- *Listening*

- *Starting and maintaining a conversation*

- *Giving and receiving compliments*

- *Introducing yourself or other people*

- *Joining in with others*

- *Using and recognizing nonverbal communication (body language, eye contact)*

While learning these social skills, many children need coaching. If your child is more inward (shy or reluctant to participate in a group setting), be prepared for him or her to acquire these skills more slowly and to tread carefully before taking action. However, even inward children need to develop social skills—shyness is not an excuse for not learning to interact successfully with others.

If you are concerned that your child may exhibit anxiety in social situations, consider seeking professional advice. Talk to your family physician or a school counselor for referrals and an assessment. There are also many things you can do to help your child feel more comfortable in a variety of social settings (or events). Barbara and Gregory Markway recommend trying to break the event down into smaller pieces that your child can relate to (see below).

> *Eric's son was nervous about his first meeting for Cub Scouts. He had no idea what to expect and the images he formed in his mind were frightening, not*

Hiroko is chatty and lo to talk at home, but wh she is around unfamilia adults or other children, she has nothing to say. Sh finds new situations tryi and her mother can't understand why Hiroko doesn't make the effort to make new friends. Her

to mention way off base. Eric was able to reassure his son, Collin, with the following pieces of information—information that broke the meeting up into smaller, more familiar pieces.

♦ "Remember the time you played at Derick's house? The meeting will be at his house, and you'll probably have a little time to play before the meeting, just like you did the other time you were there. I bet he had some neat stuff."

♦ "You've met Derick's parents before. They seemed pretty nice, didn't they? His dad is the den leader. He'll be there to tell both of us what we're going to do."

♦ "We'll probably sing some songs, play a game, and eat a snack."

(From Barbara and Gregory Markway's Web site, www.markway.com/tips/parents_encourage. For more ideas, read Nurturing the Shy Child, *by Barbara G. Markway and Gregory P. Markway.)*

 Recommended Reading

There are many good books out there about making friends that go beyond the usual, run-of-the-mill advice. Here is information about three of them; see also Children's Literature Cited, page 153.

How Do I Feel About . . . Making Friends, by Sarah Levete, is written in an interview format, using real children as models. The author asks children questions about different facets of friendship, including why friends are important, how they make friends, different kinds of friendships, and keeping friendships going. These questions are great jumping-off points for many activities for children.

How Kids Make Friends . . . Secrets for Making Lots of Friends, No Matter How Shy You Are, by Michelle Lonnie, is a great basic resource for older students (grade 3 and up) and could certainly be adapted for use with younger children. It features specific information that spells out, step by step, how to make and keep friends.

The Unwritten Rules of Friendship: Simple Strategies to Help Your Child Make Friends, by Natalie Madorsky Elman and Eileen Kennedy-Moore, teaches many of the basic social skills, using a story format. It is an excellent resource for parents.

The Markways also suggest you remind your child about his or her past successes, giving lots of encouragement and positive support, and expect your child's comfort level to increase slowly. It will take time!

Moving From Theory to Practice

As you explore these social skills with your child, he or she will need lots of opportunities to practice them. You can role-play with each other or use action figures, dolls, or puppets. Have your child practice first with you, then with siblings or relatives, and then with friends.

Learning to really listen to others and being a good conversationalist go hand in hand and develop over time. Children learn how to communicate by observing others, so by modeling good listening and conversation skills, you are helping your son or daughter to strengthen those skills.

What Does It Take to Be a Good Listener?

Being a good or engaged listener involves focusing on the person you are with, really hearing what he or she says (can you repeat what was just said?) and then asking yourself if what you've heard makes sense to you before replying. Good listeners try to respond to what they hear, rather than planning what they will say when the other person is done speaking. Some good listeners do all of these things automatically; the rest of us need to take these tips to heart.

♦ **Give your full attention** to the person who is speaking. Don't look out the window or at what else is going on in the room.

♦ **Make sure your mind is focused, too.** It can be easy to let your mind wander if you think you know what the person is going to say next—but you might be wrong! If you feel your mind wandering, change the position of your body and try to concentrate on the speaker's words.

♦ **Wait for your turn to talk.** Speakers appreciate having the chance to say everything they would like to say without being interrupted. When you interrupt, it looks as if you aren't listening, even if you really are.

♦ **Finish listening** before you begin to speak. You can't really listen if you are busy thinking about what you want to say next.

♦ **Tune in for main ideas**, the most important points the speaker wants to get across. They may be mentioned at the start or the end of a talk, and repeated a number of times. Pay special attention to statements that begin with phrases such as "My point is . . ." or "The thing to remember is . . . ."

♦ **Ask questions.** If you are not sure you understand what the speaker has said, just ask. It is a good idea to rephrase key points about what the speaker has said to clarify your understanding. For example, you might say, "When you said that no two zebras are alike, did you mean that the stripes are different on each one?"

♦ **Give feedback.** Sit up straight and look directly at the speaker. Now and then, nod to show that you understand. At appropriate points you may also smile, frown, laugh, or be silent. These are all ways to let the speaker know that you are listening carefully.

(Adapted from www.infoplease.com/homework/listeningskills1.html)

Supporting Meaningful Conversations

Children need to learn that conversations require more than one-word answers. They involve active listening to help move the conversation along. Some of the attributes of a good conversationalist include looking at the person you are talking to, using a tone of voice that indicates you're interested, providing lots of details as you speak, and smiling, nodding, laughing, and giving other cues that you are interested.

Children benefit from talking to their peers and other adults, whether it is time on the phone or by participation in social clubs, teams, or volunteer work. All of the above help give children the time to talk and build communication skills. Of course, it is important for you and your child to have some meaningful conversation, too. You don't always have to talk about school! Stuck for ideas? Here are some ideas you can use to jump-start a conversation:

♦ Discuss world events in the news (appropriate to your child's age level).

◆ Tell stories about when you were young. Encourage questions.

◆ Talk about books you are reading or want to read.

◆ Ask questions about upcoming plans, wishes, hopes, and dreams!

◆ Play word games, or tell riddles and jokes.

◆ Describe one great thing that happened that day and one terrible thing that happened that day.

Use travel time in the car or on the bus to chat about a lot of topics and catch up with one another's lives. Set aside that time as "conversation time," a time that you'll need to ban iPods, DVDs, and other distractions. If, like many families, you have conversations during shared meals, try to include discussion about a variety of topics that interest you and that interest your child. And when you have company, invite your child to greet and converse with your guests appropriately. To help set up for success, talk with your son or daughter before the guests arrive (especially if the guests are adults). Encourage your child to identify some questions to ask them. Or, invite your child to recall recent experiences he or she could share during a conversation (e.g., a lost tooth).

Model giving and receiving compliments, valuable skills to have and practice, too. You might think out loud as you consider positives about other people. (e.g., "Look at how well Evan is pitching tonight! Let's talk to him about it after the game.") And when you give compliments, they should be short, sweet, and heartfelt. (e.g., "Evan, you've been practicing your curve ball, haven't you? It really showed during the fifth inning! Way to go!") Too often, a compliment is deflected with a brush-off or denial. (e.g., "Oh, THIS old shirt? I just threw it on.") Ouch! Teach your child (and model this yourself) to respond with a simple "Thank you." A compliment is a gift, and it should be received with pride.

Decoding Body Language

Our body language affects how others see us and is a means of communication. With your child, discuss the ways in which body postures and facial expressions impact interactions between people.

Talk about the ways in which various emotions can be portrayed with nonverbal communication. (This is a time to be dramatic and have fun!) If your child is young, you might demonstrate a few easily recognizable facial expressions and then ask your child to identify feelings associated with them. For older children, take turns demonstrating feelings of happiness, sadness, anger, bewilderment, excitement, curiosity, and disinterest. Have your child name some more and try role-playing some of these. Ask: Which expressions might show someone that you liked them and might want to be friends? Which expressions might show someone that you didn't want to talk with them (e.g., looking at the ground, frowning or grimacing, turning your body away, hunching over).

> When children are asked what things make someone a good friend, they list these traits:
>
> - Cooperative
> - Helpful to others
> - Kind
> - Empathetic
> - Sharing with others
>
> (*From* Why Doesn't Anybody Like Me? A Guide to Raising Socially Confident Kids *by Hara Estroff Marano*)

Nonverbal communication has a powerful influence on human interaction. It can help bring people together, set them apart, and more. With you or with a sibling, have your child practice approaching a new friend and, without words, take turns showing that they'd like to be friends. Invite both children to take turns showing they don't want to be approached or bothered by others. Later, look for opportunities to observe the nonverbal behaviors of others in a variety of public settings (on television, at the library, at the park). Encourage your child to share his or her observations with you and discuss their probable meanings.

Putting It All Together: How to Make a Friend

Making a friend involves using key social skills. To help your child practice those skills in the comfort of home, invite him or her to imagine and talk about this scenario: Your child wants to make friends with a certain child. The potential friend is alone, but occupied. Perhaps he or she is sorting baseball cards or dribbling a basketball. Ask your child to think of behaviors that might encourage a conversation to develop. How might you get to know someone? What could you say or do? Take turns role-playing. Encourage your child to introduce himself or herself to a new friend with positive body language and statements.

On a sheet of paper, make a chart with two columns and give the chart a title, such as Making New Friends. In the first column, record your child's suggestions for positive ways to introduce himself or herself to a potential

 Recommended Reading

WHY: To introduce the topic of making friends.

How Humans Make Friends, by Loreen Leedy, is a humorous introduction to the topic. Zork Tripork, an alien, is reporting on his observations from his trip to Planet Earth. His speech is called "How Humans Make Friends" and features specific ideas on how friends meet and greet each other, things they do together, what friends talk about, how they get along, why friends don't get along, and how to solve conflict with friends.

The sections that contrast how friends get along with how they don't get along are worth focusing on. Zork mentions such things as "Friends can be trusted, friends share, friends are fair, they help each other and friends keep promises." He is just as specific talking about why friends don't get along (blabbing secrets, teasing, being selfish, acting bossy, breaking promises, acting rude).

B-E-S-T Friends, by Patricia Reilly Griff, helps children think about tolerance and empathy. Stacey has to help Annie, a new girl in school, who is different and causes problems because of her behavior. Stacey and Annie have conflicts, but unlike her classmates, Stacey recognizes that in spite of her behavior, Annie is an interesting girl. She tries to empathize with Annie, and by the end of the book they are friends.

The story helps underline the fact that we are all unique. We have qualities special to us that help make us good friends to others. Being different in some way should not be a reason to avoid being friends with someone.

Who Will Be My Friends?, by Syd Hoff, tells the story of Freddy, who is new to the neighborhood and is looking for some new friends. He asks various people (policeman, mailman) to be friends before seeing some children playing. He's unsure of how to join in, so he begins to play ball by himself. The other children see him and invite him to play ball with them.

Making New Friends

Great ways to make a friend:	Not-so-good ways to make a friend:
Smile, look the person in the eye.	Look grumpy, or look over your shoulder or at the ground.
Say "Hi!"	Don't say your name.
Ask for his or her name.	Tell the person that he or she has to play with you.
Invite the child to play a game: "Hi! My name is Claire. Do you want to play tag?"	Ignore the person when he or she is talking.
Tell the person something you like about him or her: "Wow! I really like your braids. Did you do those yourself?"	Push, hit, or kick someone to get attention.
	Run away without saying good-bye.
Offer to help with something: "Can I help you find it?"	Brag and put the other person down. "I've got one of those, too, but mine's better than yours. It was more expensive."
Mention something you like, too: "I have a favorite pen, too. Do you want to see it?"	Say something mean: "That's a really ugly shirt."
Ask for help: "Hi! My name is Jake, and I'm new here. Can you show me where to line up when recess is over?"	Fib to get someone to play with you: "The teacher said you have to play with me all the time."
	Be negative and don't try: "I can't. I don't know how. I'm scared. I don't want to do that."
	Be bossy: "You have to play the game this way. I know all the rules, and you aren't playing it right."

friend. Ask: Is it enough just to tell your name? What tone of voice will you use? What kind of body language might you see from the other child? Write down your child's ideas. When ready, have your child think of statements or actions that would not be helpful ways to make a new friend. Record those ideas in the second column. You could help your child consider scenarios with questions like: What will happen if you are bossy? What if you demand that the child participate in something you want to do? What will happen if you are loud and pushy? Interested and respectful? Take lots of time coming up with ideas and comparing them. To personalize the chart, invite your child to add illustrations or cartoons and text. You want to help make the chart a how-to resource for your child, something he or she can read and review again and again.

Your chart could look like the one on page 102.

Next, talk about how your child should react when someone comes over to introduce himself or herself. Brainstorm what your child could say. Body language is just as important here, too. Talk about what your child could do if he or she is already playing with other people. What will happen if your child just says "no" and runs off to play somewhere else? Some role-playing would be helpful here to give children a chance to experience and compare responses.

It's also important for your child to understand that he or she has a responsibility to include people in games or activities, especially children who are new to a neighborhood or to a class. No child should be excluded from games or other school activities. Plus, this is a perfect time to help your child empathize with other's feelings. Ask your child to imagine how it would feel to be standing alone on the sidelines as the other children played soccer. How would it feel if someone asked you to join? How would you feel if the other children got a birthday party invitation but you didn't? What if you received three valentines at your class party and others had 20? How would you feel if no one chose you to be on a kickball team?

Identifying Different Kinds of Friends

Children need to be able to distinguish between different types of friends, such as acquaintances and close friends. While books, videos, and even parents put a focus on having a "best" friend, children need to be able to get along and work with a wide variety of people. This leads into a discussion about types of friends. Can adults be the child's friends? Can sisters and brothers be friends? Is it best to have just one friend, or a group of friends?

A common difficulty that younger children struggle with is how to have more than one friend. Exclusivity is important to many children and is a normal part of development in children. However, we need to help children consider how this affects others. If someone asks you to play, how should you handle it if you already are playing with other people? If someone you don't like wants to be friends, how should you handle that?

This is a good time to let children know that no one should force you be friends if you don't want to be, but that even so, everyone must be treated with kindness and respect. You may want to talk about possible responses to these situations. "No, thanks. I am reading right now so I can't play with you. But thank you for asking me" or "I'm sorry, but I can't go to your party. That's nice that you wanted to ask me" are respectful ways of saying no without hurting someone's feelings.

Your child also needs to think about the kinds of people he or she would like to be friends with. Encourage your son or daughter to observe people he or she would like to be friendly with before making an introduction. Does the potential friend treat others with kindness? Is he or she bossy or mean to others? Does the person try to make others do things that are not right? (Inward or shy children often do this filtering of "Who is safe and who isn't" naturally.)

Invite your child to consider this question: Can a person be friends with anyone? This leads into a good discussion about empathy, acceptance, and suitability, which may in turn help your child realize that anyone can be a friend as long as that person supports your being happy, comfortable, and safe.

Walking in Someone Else's Shoes

Empathizing with others is a skill every one of us needs to work on developing. To help your child practice thinking about how others feel and understanding how people's feelings can impact their actions and reactions, consider the suggestions that follow.

♦ **If you have babies or toddlers in your home, or relatives who are infants, encourage older children to interact with them, and to interpret the emotions and behaviors they see.** For example, if an older child takes away a toy the baby is playing with, ask what they think the baby is feeling. If you had a toy taken away from you, what would you feel? What would you do? How would you communicate your feelings?

♦ **Discuss comics, magazines, and books your child reads.** The act of "reading between the lines" and interpreting a character's thoughts and motivations through his or her actions is an integral part of reading comprehension, too. If your child has a difficult time with this, have him or her role-play scenarios from the story. Viewing a character's body language helps younger children understand how emotions and actions may affect the next event.

Pointing out conflict between characters or in interactions your children have with peers also gives children a chance to empathize with others. Resolving conflict with others is another essential social skill. Any conflict situation that you and your children deal with must involve an opportunity for all of the children involved to share their thoughts and feelings. (You can learn more about working through conflict in Chapter Six.)

♦ **Developing tolerance, empathy, and respect for others must be ongoing.** To help your child develop these skills, look for opportunities to give them the satisfaction of helping others—and give your child as many opportunities as possible to interact positively with as many others (including you!) as possible, in both your school and your community.

• Get your child involved in scouting, church groups, or clubs with a special interest; look for groups that don't necessarily focus on individual progress (for example, swimming lessons) but on group achievements (a synchronized swimming group). This helps foster a feeling of belonging to a group. Music lessons are a great way to build up a child's skills and feelings of accomplishment, but joining a singing group or children's orchestra puts the focus on friendship and working together for a common cause.

• Participate as a family in community events. This will have a huge impact on your child's ability to meet and get to know many new people from many different walks of life. Volunteering at a food bank, taking part in a park cleanup, getting involved in a community project, helping out in an election campaign—all of these allow children to feel good about themselves, see that they can have a positive impact on their community, and, hopefully, meet some new friends.

To learn more about the role of empathy and how it relates to bullying, turn to page 86 in Chapter Four.

The Roots of Empathy

"Empathy is the ability to identify with another person's feelings. The ability to see and feel things as others see and feel them is central to . . . successful social relationships in all stages of life. When children are able to understand another person's point of view and respect their feelings, aggressive behavior is less likely to occur."

The Roots of Empathy is a hugely successful program that visits inner city schools in Toronto, Canada. It's a big part of many anti-bullying programs. Throughout the school year, facilitators for the program bring infants into classrooms along with their caregivers. Children in the classroom "learn the names of the feelings as the baby's cues are interpreted." Schools that participate in the program find that "because children are taught empathy, and are encouraged to take responsibility for their actions and inactions . . . incidents of bullying fall." (www.rootsofempathy.org)

Nobody roots for Goliath.

~Wilt Chamberlain,
former NBA star

Compassion is the basis
of all morality.

~Arthur Schopenhauer,
German philosopher

 **CHAPTER SIX**

Conflict Resolution

In this chapter, you will learn a simple, effective, and down-to-earth strategy that helps your child learn how to successfully resolve conflicts with others. This set of easy-to-follow steps is called conflict resolution. These steps help you step back from the enforcer role and help your child learn how to solve problems fairly and quickly.

As we discussed in Chapter One, bullying and conflict are often mistaken for each other. Bullying is about power; conflict rears its ugly head anywhere that people live or work together. Our role as adults is to prepare children for the "real world," and a huge part of that world means dealing with others successfully. Learning appropriate social skills, as mentioned in Chapter Five, is vital to a child's healthy development. Learning how to resolve problems with others successfully is one momentous piece of that puzzle.

Why is conflict resolution so helpful in bullying situations? I quickly realized the potential of this strategy to minimize bullying because it holds children accountable for their behavior. Bullies don't like their behavior to be out in the open. They don't want to be face to face with the child they're bullying, to have to listen to how their actions affected another person in negative ways. As well, bullies realize that they will be confronted and held responsible for their actions. Bullies benefit from learning to deal with conflict in a constructive way. Vulnerable children, too, benefit immensely from being able to confront their tormentor in a controlled, safe setting.

> As Carla Garrity wrote, "Remember, vulnerability attracts aggressors. Helping the children work for small gains that nurture their confidence and strength will be beneficial." (From *Bully-Proofing Your School*, 2004.)

Small gains are so important. They offer opportunities for children to feel successful and capable: "I can handle this, and I know what to do." If a child is at the park and his friend takes his basketball and he is able to confront him, talk about what the friend did and how he felt about it, then come to a solution they both agreed to—that's empowering. Issues that are not life-and-death situations can provide opportunities for constructive problem solving.

- ◆ Children who feel successful and capable of solving minor problems are more likely to stand up for themselves and learn to handle conflict appropriately in general.

- ◆ Children who are confident problem-solvers are not as intimidated by aggression or the threatening behavior of bullies. Rather, they understand the process of dealing with the problem with the other student, relying on adults to act as coaches rather than solvers. They take ownership of the problem, and agree to a solution that works for the people involved.

Bottom line? Bullies quickly learn that they will be held accountable for their behavior and they experience firsthand the effect their actions had upon another. They also learn that the child they harassed is willing and able to stand up for himself or herself and will not be a silent target. Bullies learn a lot via conflict resolution skills!

Benefits on All Sides

Like many parents, you probably can relate to the frequent bickering and arguments between siblings or friends, and it often seems easier to jump in and resolve the problem for them—but that comes at the expense of children becoming responsible problem-solvers themselves.

Children tend not to take ownership of their problems or buy into the resolution if they know they don't have a voice in fixing the problem, and their lack of ownership can cause three negative behavior patterns.

♦ They may routinely rely on others to fix their problems, rather than manage them independently. A child who relies on others loses the ability to think or learn to problem-solve appropriately, which will impact every single area of his or her life when an adult. And, having others jump in and solve your problems also sends you the message that you can't handle things yourself. Feelings of incompetence undermine a sense of self-esteem, and that's the last thing a timid or passive child needs to experience. In fact, these are the children that well-meaning adults often rush in to help, the very children who need to learn conflict resolution skills the most!

♦ Children who depend on adults to solve problems often become angry and complain that they aren't listened to or treated fairly, and this anger can become a behavior issue.

♦ Without a chance to resolve his or her own conflicts, a child will seek other ways of taking control, including bullying others, to feel the power they are denied.

In short, dealing with various kinds of conflict is something all children need to learn.

Defining Conflict Resolution

During my first few years of teaching, I realized that unless I enabled children to take responsibility for solving conflict themselves, I was doomed to spend much of my classroom teaching time solving others' problems. I was looking for answers and I found them in conflict resolution. Let's begin by defining what conflict resolution is.

Conflict resolution is a way people can talk out problems with others. In conflict resolution, each person has the chance to tell his or her side of the story, how it made them feel, and, with your help, decide how to solve the problem.

Conflict resolution skills focus on allowing children to take ownership of problem solving in a safe environment. It is not a new concept, and it is slowly becoming more visible in school settings. I liked the logical and straightforward structure, tried it, and developed my own easy, four-step framework for problem solving that works. As with bully-proofing, the best place to introduce these skills is with younger children, but they certainly work with older children, too.

The model introduced here is highly structured; you'll help children practice solving problems, large and small, with others as you talk, role-play, read books about conflict resolution, and consistently use this problem-solving format in your daily life. By following these steps, your child will become skilled at identifying the main issue, calmly discussing it, and working together to come up with a resolution that is satisfactory to all. You become a coach, not the "resolver/ enforcer" of arguments or dis-agreements.

As you use these steps with your child each and every time there is a problem to resolve (consistency is the key!), you may be frustrated with how long it takes to settle issues that, in the past, you ended quickly by stepping in and deciding the outcome yourself. While it may seem to make your life easier to be the enforcer, resist the urge to be one! Your child will catch on quickly. The more you go through the steps, the faster using them successfully will become a habit, and the rewards are huge. In my classroom, children invariably developed such confidence that by the end of the year most, if not all, problems that developed were dealt with quickly and successfully by the children with little input from me.

> Keep in mind that the conflict resolution strategies I describe aren't right for every situation, especially conflict situations that involve physical aggression. When children are in danger, feel threatened, or are involved in patterns of bullying behavior, you have to intervene more actively. In general, however, your ultimate goal should be to enable your child to become comfortable with talking out minor, everyday problems and taking ownership of the problem-solving process.

Taking Responsibility for Solving Problems

To begin introducing your child to conflict resolution, talk about how important it is for people to be able to work out problems with others. You could ask: What happens when adults solve problems for you? If you are angry with someone, should you ignore that person and/or explain how you feel? What are some actions that would help solve a problem with someone? Your child should be able to give some practical suggestions, including talking, asking an adult to help, and letting a bully know that you are upset. If you ask what are some behaviors that would not help solve a problem, your child might identify crying, yelling, hitting, and saying "I don't care."

Moving forward, your son or daughter may come to realize that there are many ways of solving a problem so that everyone involved feels satisfied. To underscore the point, you might share some books of fiction. From simple picture books to chapter books, these character-driven conflicts can give you the opportunity to use stories you read with your child as a springboard for talking about being angry, whether or not the characters handle the problem successfully, and the many ways people can feel when they don't like the way someone else has treated them.

 Recommended Reading

WHY: To show that there are many different ways to solve a problem

READ: *I Want It* by Elizabeth Crary

In this story, Megan and Amy are playing together. Amy wants to play with a toy that Megan has, and she considers seven different ways she can get the toy, some better than others. Since it's written in a "Story Tree" format, the readers make the decisions and see the consequences of each choice.

The book includes questions about feelings and making decisions as each alternative is considered. It's designed to be read with a parent or teacher, and the pages in the back summarize these ideas/choices.

Using the Anger Escalator Strategy

Anger is the one emotion that most children will automatically associate with conflict, so this is an ideal time to discuss anger and how it can build . . . and build.

The "Anger Escalator" (Teolis, 1998) is an excellent image for children to use when they are angry. Photocopy the reproducible graphic on page 113 and use it to stimulate conversations about how escalators can go up and down. Think aloud, inviting your child to consider how people go up the escalator and how this relates to people becoming angry. Ask: As you go up each step and get angrier and angrier, what happens? How do you feel at each step? How does your body feel as you get angry? As you get angrier, what happens to your body language? Your voice? The way you act?

Invite your child to think about how he or she can go down the Anger Escalator. Taking a deep breath, counting to ten, walking away from the situation until you are calmer, and consciously clenching and relaxing your arms, legs, and other body parts are all good ways to begin to bring the emotion under control. You could certainly relate this to the Breathe Deep! strategy described in Chapter Three.

Some children do have difficulty calming down, whether excited or upset. Talking about effective strategies and having your child think about the escalator image really helps teach realistic ways of learning to control emotions. Remember, the goal here is not to eliminate the feeling, just to control it. Emphasize repeatedly that experiencing emotions is normal and often helpful to us as human beings. It's how we *handle* our emotions that makes a difference in how we are perceived by others.

To help your child think about the anger escalator strategy in action, create a visual reminder that shows how feelings can build up and then dissipate. Begin by making a copy of the reproducible Anger Escalator graphic on page 113. Add details to it with your child. Where the stairs go up, add words or pictures to describe the feelings that go with them and the intensity of those steps. Where the stairs descend, add details about how a person can calm down when angry. (This same elevator format can be used to chart other emotions your child may experience with bullying, such as fear and anxiety.)

Anger Escalator

Think about your emotions like steps on an escalator that rise and then drop. On the face beside each step, draw how you feel when you're angry and then when you're calming down. On the lines, write about it. If you get stuck, you can ask yourself, "How did I feel at first?" and "How did I feel afterward?"

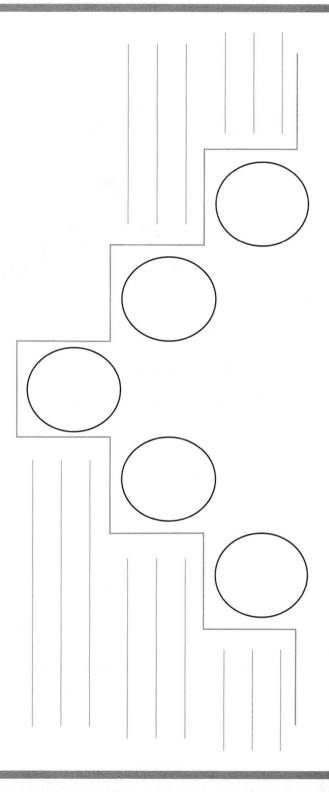

What a younger child might create:

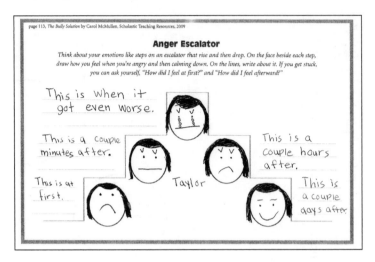

What an older child might create:

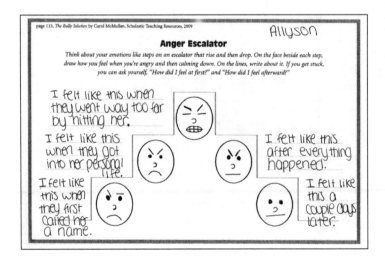

After your child has explored identifying feelings of anger and ways of calming down, you're ready to help your child learn the steps to solving the conflicts he or she faces.

Four Steps to Resolving a Problem

With your child, look at the box below and talk about the steps he or she will take in situations where conflict resolution is needed. You can create your own version to hang in a prominent place. Remember that visuals like these help children (and you!) remember what needs to be done.

Each step is integral in a successful conflict resolution situation. You, as the parent, need to be aware that there is a problem and be ready to coach the children through all the steps.

To solve a problem, I will take these steps:

1. Tell an adult we need to resolve a problem.

2. Use our "My Turn" statements to give each person a chance to tell his or her side of the story.

3. Decide on a solution that is fair for both people.

4. Shake hands.

STEP 1. Telling an adult may also help de-escalate an angry situation from spiraling out of control, because having to physically go to a parent allows each child time to take a break from the conflict and begin calming down.

Take a few minutes to reiterate the difference between tattling and telling (see sidebar). If a child comes to me and begins to complain about another person's behavior, I ask him or her to think about whether this is tattling or telling. I let them know that if they

The Difference Between Tattling and Telling

Try sharing these definitions with your child before he or she commences a story about what happened to whom.

Tattling: If it will only get another person into trouble, don't tell me.

Telling: If it will get you or another child out of trouble, tell me.

If it is both (tattling and telling), I need to know.

(Adapted from *The Bully, the Bullied, and the Bystander* by Barbara Coloroso, 2003, p. 135)

have a problem to work out with someone, that person needs to be involved. Never allow children to pour out their story before the other person has joined the meeting.

STEP 2. **Making "My Turn" statements** allows each person to have his or her say, not be interrupted, and gives him or her the confidence each will be heard and treated fairly. Help your child understand that you will not allow him or her to simply complain about a problem he or she is having with someone, and that all parties involved must be included from the beginning.

Some "My Turn" statements that your child can use in every problem-solving situation include:

♦ Tell _____ what the problem is.

♦ Tell _____ how that made you feel. (How do you think it made the other person feel?)

♦ Tell _____ what you want him/her to do next time.

Teach your child to always use these statements word for word. They are the framework for solving most problems. It's essential to use exactly the same words and processes each time so they become a habit. If using different words, children can step off-track and be distracted from successfully talking out the issue.

STEP 3. **Deciding on a solution** that is fair is often the simplest part of the process! By this point, each child should be calmer and able to think about the consequences of the conflict.

STEP 4. **Shaking hands** signals the end of the problem, and that it will not be revisited in the future.

Body Language and Behavioral Expectations

Body language also plays a role in successful problem solving. You may choose to do some role-playing to show how looking at the floor, mumbling, slouching, crossing your arms, or yelling at someone can negatively affect how the problem is solved.

Make your body language and behavior expectations clear and highlight that they play a valuable role in solving a problem and bringing an end to a bullying situation. Consider listing these expectations on a sheet of paper and posting it where your child can easily see and review it.

The guidelines below can be used any time people are trying to communicate with one another. When talking out a problem, a person should . . .

Look at the other person's face and into their eyes.

Talk in a calm, clear voice. Don't mumble.

Stand up straight and face the other person.

Stay engaged. Saying "I don't know" is not allowed.

Discuss some reasons why engagement during the problem-solving process is important. Why is saying "I don't know" not allowed? Explain that children who use that phrase are "copping out" instead of dealing with a conflict situation cooperatively and honestly. Take turns role-playing examples of how saying "I don't know" can roadblock any attempt to solve a problem.

We need to teach children how to speak and communicate effectively all the time. The body language guidelines listed above help that happen.

Guiding Children Through Discussion

Your job during conflict resolution is to act as a coach, asking the guiding questions and keeping the discussion on track.

Here is a typical problem that you might encounter. Notice how the parent in this scenario focuses the discussion, keeps the two children on track, and offers solutions.

Bill and his friend John are yelling at each other as they come into the kitchen.

Bill: Mom, John stole my comic!

John: I didn't!

Mom: Okay boys, let's sit down here at the kitchen table and talk.

John: Look, I already told you I won't take it again.

Mom: John, our rule is that you two need to do some conflict resolution. Bill, tell John what the problem is.

Bill: The problem is that you stole my Nintendo comic and you just took it off my desk without even asking me.

John: I couldn't because . . . .

Mom: John, it's Bill's turn to talk. You need to listen right now. Bill, tell John how that made you feel.

Bill: I felt really mad because you didn't even ask me, you just took it. And it hurt my feelings, too.

Mom: Tell John what you want him to do next time.

Bill: Next time I want you to ask me before you take it and not steal it.

Mom: John, tell Bill about this problem.

John: Well, I needed something to read and you said I could read it last week and I couldn't ask you 'cause you took so long in the bathroom and I looked at it for a minute but I forgot to give it back and I put it in my backpack to keep it safe and I never stole it.

Mom: John, how did you feel when you took his comic?

John: Okay, because I was only borrowing it. If I was really stealing it, I would feel mad at him.

Mom: John, how do you think Bill felt?

John: Well, angry at me, I guess.

Mom: Tell Bill what you will do next time.

John: I won't take your comic, I'll wait for you to come back.

Mom: Are there any other choices you could make next time?

John: I guess I could take another book to read, but I wouldn't like it as much as the Nintendo one.

Mom: Hmmm, what about your book from school that you are taking home to read? Could you have chosen that one, instead of taking the Nintendo comic?

John: Yeah, I guess. But it's a boring book. I'd rather read the Nintendo.

Mom: Do you have any other choices? What could you have done to make sure you didn't forget to give the book back?

John: Well, I guess I shouldn't have put it in my backpack because that's why I forgot I had it. So next time I could just read it sitting on Bill's bed.

Mom: Bill, do you have your comic back?

Bill: Yep.

Mom: Is the problem solved? Are you friends again?

John and Bill: Yeah, friends again.

Mom: Okay, shake on it and, John, please remind us what you will do next time.

John: (shaking hands) Sorry, Bill. Next time I will read my own book or read yours sitting on your bed and not put it in my backpack.

Mom: Great job. Problem solved. Would you guys like some milk and cookies?

–end–

Supporting the Process Step by Step

STEP 1: The first step is for the children to let you know there is a problem to be resolved. When you have gathered the children involved, make sure they are calm enough to resolve the problem. Explain that during the conflict resolution process:

♦ everyone involved is given the courtesy of being heard

♦ no one is allowed to interrupt or shortchange someone when it's his or her turn to speak. Let the participants know that they will have their chance to speak. Now it's time for them to really listen.

Most of the time, children settle down quickly, especially when they know that they will have equal time to share their side of the story and their feelings. There's no point in going through the process if your child is extremely upset or crying. If this is the case, ask both children to go to separate areas for a few minutes until they are ready to calmly talk out the problem. Some children initially have difficulty settling themselves down, but they learn to do so quickly when they are in a "time out" situation and do not receive any attention or interest that may fuel their emotions.

STEP 2: Ask your child to begin. Prompt your child to speak directly to the other child.

"Tell John what the problem is." Expect your child to repeat the same language as they describe the problem.

"The problem is that you stole my Nintendo comic and you just took it off my desk without even asking me."

In the beginning, children will look at you and tell you what happened. Gently remind them that you didn't cause their problem. They need to remember to talk to the person they have the problem with. Some children have great difficulty with this, but by allowing them to complain to you, you are in effect setting yourself up as the judge, not the coach.

Do not accept a statement that is vague. For example, "You were being mean to me" tells the other person nothing about the problem. Expect children to be specific: "Tell John *exactly* what he did that is a problem for you." "The problem is you stole my Nintendo comic and you just took it off my desk without even asking me."

Prompt the child to clearly state his or her feelings about the situation. "Tell John how that made you feel."

"I felt really mad because you didn't even ask me, you just took it. And it hurt my feelings, too."

Give children "think" time; a few seconds of silence gives children a chance to organize their thoughts. If they appear to be unsure of what to say, it's okay to ask them further questions to bring out how they feel.

Finally, use the prompt "Tell John what you want him to do next time."

It is a great way to have children think about solutions, and restitution, if necessary.

"Next time I want you to ask me before you take it and not steal it.

Now it's the other child's turn to go through the same three questions. The second question should be varied a bit to include the action the child took that caused the problem. **"John, how did you feel when you took his comic? How do you think Bill felt?"** These questions are essential to help develop empathy.

The response from the second child can often be quite revealing; it's not unusual for the accused child to be reacting to a grievance he or she harbors from a previous incident. For example, a variation of this situation could be that John took Bill's comic because Bill took John's racing car without asking. Discovering this information allows you to have children deal with both issues, and emphasizes that not dealing with small problems can lead to bigger ones.

STEP 3: Agree upon a solution that works for both children. Both participants need a solution that can be lived with. Often children know what to do and come up readily with ideas. They must understand that the solution has to be linked to the original problem and be appropriate. Be sure they realize that, while the solution is their decision, you must agree with it. This ensures that unreasonable or impractical solutions are not accepted. ("I want Ryan to stay up until midnight every day for two months to make up for yelling at me!")

Have children apologize and tell what he or she will do the next time. "Sorry, Bill. Next time I will read my own book or read yours sitting on your bed" is all that's necessary. If children have difficulty coming up with a solution, lay out various ways they can resolve a problem and then have them agree on the one they feel will work. Notice how the parent in the scenario is careful to only make suggestions and not indicate the right choice (for her!). She says, "Are there any other choices you could make next time? Do you have any other choices? What could you have done . . . ?"

Try as hard as you can not to influence their decision; you are simply there to provide the choices. Be careful! It's easy to unwittingly impose your preference ("Of course, *the easiest thing to do* would be to just not touch any of Bill's things until Bill is there.") It's not up to you to decide what's best for them.

When both children are comfortable with the solution, I will often use a bit of drama and "hit the rewind button!" I have them act out the original problem with the new solution. I push a spot on their foreheads, make a whirring sound, and then say, "Try again." Kids love this step, and it's a

In some situations, restitution (replacing or fixing what was done) is appropriate. The restitution should be reasonable and follow logically as a consequence of the problem. Here are some examples:

The Problem	*The Restitution*
A stolen piece of Halloween candy	Replacing it with a piece from your own stash
A drawing that was torn	Taping up the paper carefully
Orange juice spilled on homework	A note written to the teacher by the spiller explaining the problem
A piece of borrowed clothing returned dirty	Clothing being cleaned by borrower
A favorite pencil stolen	Replacement with pencil of equal value

quick indicator that they've understood the problem and can demonstrate how they will handle it next time. Usually this ends in smiles, which is a nice way to lead into the last step, shaking hands.

STEP 4: **When the children shake hands**, the situation is resolved and they must agree not to refer to it again.

While the explanation sounds long and detailed, you'll be surprised that the actual conflict resolution rarely takes more than a few minutes from start to finish when children become used to the process.

That small amount of time results in huge rewards for your children. Confident, capable problem-solvers tend not to be the targets of bullies, and children who bully also benefit by experiencing the real-life consequences of their behaviors. When they are expected to assume responsibility for their behavior, bullies recognize and experience the feelings of others and learn to empathize through this process. It also holds them accountable for making amends and provides an opportunity to think about and practice more acceptable behavior in the future. As a further bonus, they may experience a positive feeling when their apology is accepted. Laughter and a handshake go a long way toward making everyone feel equal and valued.

Children who are bullied are exposed to an excellent modeling process

Practice makes perfect! Try role-playing these situations with your child to give him or her a chance to work through the steps. This also gives him or her a chance to begin thinking about reasonable, appropriate solutions and restitution.

Person A *has the grievance* and **Person B** *is the accused.*

Person A is sad because **Person B** laughed at a picture she drew for school.

Person A is angry because **Person B**, without permission, knocked down the block tower **Person A** built.

Person A is upset because **Person B** took the last chocolate chip cookie from the plate that was supposed to be for **Person A**.

Person A is furious because **Person B** spilled orange juice on **Person A**'s homework.

You and your child will be able to come up with many other scenarios!

as they learn to express themselves and experience a satisfactory resolution in a safe, supportive environment that recognizes the views of *all* of the people involved. Led by a caring parent, bullies and bullied children alike will gain from a conflict resolution process that treats everyone respectfully, inclusively, and sympathetically.

The Internet is just a world passing around notes in a classroom.

~Jon Stewart
comedian

CHAPTER SEVEN

Cyber Bullying

Bullying has been with us since time began, but this new form of bullying has exploded over the past several years. Cyber bullying is now a huge issue, fanned by the proliferation of technology that is easily accessible not only to the average adult, but to children as well.

> *Cyber bullying is willful and repeated harm inflicted through the media of electronic text.* (Patchin and Hinduja, 2006)

While it's tempting for us to believe that cyber bullying occurs only among adolescents, the truth is that younger children are more often becoming targets or perpetrators.

In this chapter, we will explore the various ways that technology can be used to harass others, but more important, it will give you the best ways of protecting your child and family from online bullying. The problem seems enormous, and if you aren't that

My daughter is so upset. She's been getting e-mails from someone accusing her of all sorts of hurtful and untrue things, and threatening to beat her up. The worst thing is, she gets these e-mails all the time and we can't figure out who it is. It's a frightening feeling to be threatened in your own home by

familiar with computers, it may seem impossible to really do much. The truth is that there are many simple, easy things you can do, no matter what your level of expertise.

Risks and Realities

Our children have been raised in the technology age and, unlike many parents, are completely comfortable with computers, the Internet, the World Wide Web, e-mail, text-messaging, camera phones, and file downloading and sharing. Many adults, myself included, have difficulty figuring out how to turn on our cell phones and answer a call, let alone send e-mails or access information that children can retrieve in a split second.

Most children today are taught keyboarding skills and how to use the Internet at school; e-mailing others and using school networks are commonplace. By third grade, children often are creating Web sites and PowerPoint presentations. They have their own cell phones (with cameras) and e-mail accounts.

Yet, with all their familiarity with the technology, most children and their parents do not understand the realities and risks of being a part of the computer/cell-phone world. Children may be able to use the technology easily, but they lack the life skills, maturity, and experience to use it wisely.

Over and over, statistics indicate that as many as 85 percent of children online are completely unsupervised by an adult. And those same children say that their computers are located in their bedrooms, they have no home

Did you see that video on Facebook? The one about the teacher who loses it and starts yelling and screaming? Well, it said on the news that the students, two 13-year-old girls who didn't like him, set it up. One girl provoked the teacher and the other one filmed it on her cell phone camera and then they put it on the Web. Now he's off on stress leave. I heard the announcer say that this is called

I got a call from my son's teacher, asking me to come in after school. When I arrived, she told me my son had been involved in a bullying incident —and he was the bully! Apparently, the teacher has set up a class Web site that allows kids in the class to e-mail each other, I guess a sort of network. But instead of talking about homework, my son wrote some nasty things to a girl

RESEARCH

IN THE

Software Savvy

In a study conducted by Cox Communications and the National Center for Missing and Exploited Children in 2005, parents reported that "over half (51 percent) of parents either do not have, or do not know if they have, software on their computer(s) that monitors where their teenager(s) go online and with whom they interact. Almost half (49 percent) of parents either do not have, or do not know if they have, software on their computer that blocks specific Web sites or key words." (Parents Internet Monitoring Study, Cox Communications with the National Centre for Missing and Exploited Children, February 2005).

rules for using the Internet or chat rooms, and their parents rarely or never ask questions or drop by to see what they are doing online. ("Young Canadians in a Wired World: The Student's View," October 2001, Environics Research)

Of course, computers are extremely valuable, and the Internet, cell phones, and text messaging can be positive things. Research for school projects, educational sites, word processing, and e-mails that connect with family and friends are all wonderful tools to access from a home computer. Cell phones can be valuable ways to keep in touch with children during the day and especially useful for children if there are emergencies.

Spotting Cyber Bullying

The dark side of technology has recently exploded with the advent of cyber bullying. This new aspect of bullying is especially troubling because it is hidden, anonymous, and faceless; unlike regular bullying, cyber bullying is even more threatening to children (and parents) because it is difficult, if not impossible, to identify the bully and take steps to deal with the bullying. Using temporary e-mail accounts and pseudonyms make online bullies harder to find. By sending messages that are most often received on home computers or Internet-connected cell phones, the bully invades the target's home, personal space, and privacy and leaves him or her feeling vulnerable and attacked, with no safe place to be; the harassment can take place 24/7. As well, some bullies post their activities on the Internet, so bullied children can be "out there" in cyberspace with no control or recourse when their personal information is released or they are ridiculed or harassed. In fact, the role of bystanders takes on new dimensions in the digital world; numerous individuals have the opportunity to join in with the bullying.

There are many other ways to bully someone online. Cyber-bullying strategies include:

♦ sending e-mails containing insults or threats

♦ rumors

♦ hurtful messages

♦ embarrassing photographs taken by cell-phone cameras

♦ creating a fake Web site set up in the target child's name, in which the bully reveals untrue information

♦ building a Web site to target someone

♦ using stolen passwords to send out threats to others using the target child's name or e-mail

♦ using the target child's assumed identity to sign them up for e-mail, pornography, or other spam

♦ "happy slapping" (taking photos of set-up bullying situations and then posting them online)

RESEARCH IN THE

Proximity Matters

In an AOL study, more than half of the parents surveyed think the Internet is safe for kids, but nearly 20 percent of their children under 13 say they've been bullied online. The survey also showed that 83 percent of parents are not present when their children are online, and have no idea what Internet-safe policies are in effect at their child's school or libraries. (AOL Canada, *Internet Online Safety Week*, Leger Marketing, May 2006)

In a 2005 survey conducted by Sameer Hinduja and Justin Patchin, 1,500 young people were asked about cyber-bullying. Thirty-two percent of males and 36 percent of females reported being bullied. The most common ways they were bullied were through chat rooms (56 percent), instant messaging (49 percent), and e-mail (28 percent). Forty percent felt they were disrespected and 12 percent were threatened. (Patchin & Hinduja, 2006)

Apart from the bullying aspect, a secondary issue, as noted by a Quebec teen bully (see page 128), is that postings can be distributed in seconds.

In Action: Worldwide Teasing

In Quebec, Canada, a high school student became the target of worldwide teasing and ridicule when three of his schoolmates found a video of him pretending to be a Star Wars hero. Unbeknownst to him, they made copies and circulated his image online.

"I wanted (the boy) to know what I knew of him, what I had seen . . . to pull a joke on (him)," said one of the boys involved.

After a month, one U.S. Web blog that had posted the video reported that the clip had been downloaded over a million times and was also shown around the world on television. The boy's lawyer said in a court filing, ". . . that the video was so widely circulated that one Internet site solely dedicated to the two-minute clip recorded 76 million visits by October, 2004." ("Star Wars Kid Cuts a Deal With His Tormentors," Tu Thanh Ha, *Globe and Mail*, April 7, 2006)

The boy sued his tormentors, and in court transcripts he related how the bullying had left him unable to attend school. "It was unbearable, totally. It was impossible to attend class." He said he was diagnosed with depression and eventually left the school to work with a private tutor. Wherever he went, people would call to him and taunt him about being the Star Wars kid.

When confronted, his main tormentor said, "It's no fun, what happened here, but that's the problem with the Internet. Things travel fast." (Ibid, April 7, 2006)

Three years later, the teen and his parents reached an out-of-court settlement in the case.

And there are no guarantees that the things you put online, either in chat rooms, on Web sites, or in e-mail messages, will stay private.

In fact, in one study completed by Microsoft Canada, 70 percent of children ages 10 to 14 who use the Internet believe that the information they post and send to friends is private. "There's a feeling that kids don't view the Internet as a physical space. When they're there, they're bullet-proof and they can do no wrong and they can't be harmed." says Gavin Thompson, director of community affairs at Microsoft Canada. (Ipsos Reid: Microsoft Canada, December 2006)

Terms You Need to Know

CHATROOM An area in a site where you can chat with other members in real time. You generally must register to be able to chat with others.

BLOG It is the short form of Web log or online diary.

EMOTICONS The little faces you may see in e-mails and text messages. They are created using the Shift key and various keystrokes to create the emoticon, such as :^0 or :^)

GAMING SITES These popular sites feature games that can be played individually or with others online.

ISP Internet service provider, or the company you use to access your Internet and e-mail accounts.

JAVA A computer programming language specifically designed for creating programs that can be safely downloaded from the Internet that will not allow viruses to harm your computer or files.

POP-UP A new window that suddenly "pops up" on your screen. Sometimes a pop-up will be information from a program you are using; it's also often an ad that appears when you are on a Web site.

SOCIAL NETWORKING SITES These sites create an online community where people can share their lives with others using a profile. Profiles can include videos, blogs, and photo albums, and all give basic personal information about the user. These Web sites also allow friends to communicate directly with each other. Facebook and MySpace are popular sites of this kind.

VIRTUAL REALITY OR WORLD The simulation of a real or imagined environment that can be experienced in three dimensions and also provides an interactive experience with sound and touch and other forms of feedback, making it feel as if you are actually in another place experiencing the scenario.

> *The two cardinal rules for being in a chat room:*
> *Everyone is a stranger.*
> *Everyone lies.*
>
> ~CONSTABLE KATHY MACDONALD, CYBER BULLYING EXPERT
> CALGARY POLICE SERVICE'S CRIME PREVENTION UNIT

Concerns About Chat Rooms and Web Cams

Chat rooms, where children discuss topics in real time, run the gamut in terms of subjects; gaming chat rooms and other topics likely to appeal to young people are popular choices. Many of these chat rooms are not monitored; moderators at each site generally do not restrict the conversation and assume no responsibility for the topics discussed.

Add to this situation children's tendency to view the people they talk to online as being friends and to take everything that is presented at face value.

You must make sure that your child understands that your real-world rules such as not talking to strangers must transfer to the virtual world. It's essential for children to realize that you just don't know who you are really talking to, no matter who they say they are.

Along with chat rooms often go Web cams. These small, innocuous-looking cameras sit on top of your computer and transmit live images. With a camera such as this, you are inviting strangers into the privacy of

©2007 by Daniel Shelton

RESEARCH

IN THE

Sixty percent of children have used chat rooms and instant messaging, and one in three 9- and 10-year-olds visit chat rooms regularly. (Environics Research, October 2001)

your home. Through live images sent via Web cams, predators have greater access to children, and it's no surprise that we hear about many examples of young girls being bullied into sexual acts played out for a "friend" online.

The bottom line is, while this tool has some valuable uses, such as communicating with grandparents or other relatives, it can easily be turned into a tool for bullies and predators. **Never allow a Web cam to be used in a child's bedroom or without supervision.**

With all of these frightening stories and statistics, coupled with the lack of understanding we as adults have about the technology itself, and the speed at which new technologies with potential methods of bullying are introduced, it may be tempting to sever our ties with all digital services and try to avoid cyber bullying and other abuses altogether.

Instead, there are many things you can do to deal with cyber bullying, and many places you can go for further information and support.

Navigating the Internet Safely

The simplest, most effective way to help your children avoid being bullied, or prevent them from bullying others online, is to make sure your home computer is in a high-traffic area. Computers *with Internet access* should never be in bedrooms, basements, or other areas that don't offer you constant easy access and the ability to see what sites your child is accessing, whom they are chatting with, and what kinds of materials he or she is being exposed to, willingly or unwillingly.

As a parent, you must make yourself aware of where your children go and what they do online, and be aware of possible hazards of unlimited and unsupervised computer use. Here are some simple ways to Internet-monitor your children:

♦ Let your child know that he or she will be monitored. Some parents (and many children!) consider this snooping, but most experts agree that children should realize that they will never have privacy online. Everything they send or say is out of their control once they hit

Send, and their messages can be viewed (and used) by anyone, and will probably exist on the Internet forever—there is no time limit on postings. The Internet and e-mail are not the same as a diary. If everybody else in the world sees it, then why can't you?

♦ Set rules and draw up a simple contract for Internet use to be followed by everyone in the family, adults included. The rules should be posted next to the computer for all to see, and every computer user must sign the bottom. For examples of contracts and rules, see Appendix A.

♦ As with schoolyard bullying, talk about and make a plan detailing what your child will do when faced with a bullying situation online. For example, you and your child could agree that, if faced with a bullying message online (or anything else that makes them uncomfortable), he or she should:

1. Not respond (even if what the person is saying is not true).

2. Save the message right away.

3. Tell you or another responsible adult.

4. Together, block the sender (in your e-mail program, click on options and then go to the junk mail filter).

5. Report the message to the Internet service provider.

Another example of a personal plan is included later in this chapter, on page 139.

By using some basic strategies, you can give yourself the tools you'll need to help if cyber bullying occurs. They include:

♦ **Know your child's username, login, and passwords to the sites they visit.** Keeping a log of these should be a part of your contract (see Appendix A). Require your child to have you present when they register on a new site. A sample Web Site Log that you could use is found in Appendix D.

♦ **Have your child change passwords frequently.** This is especially important if you believe someone may have gained access to them.

- **Keep close tabs on Web pages your child may create.** Photographs are not safe online, and personal information such as a child's full name, address, age, school attended, and so on should never be used. Make sure your children's friends do not post personal information about your child on their Web site; you can visit their Web sites to check.

- **Use a family-friendly search engine** such as www.dibdabdoo.com or www.ajkids.com, and make it your home page. On the Google home page, you can click your preferences (to the right of the search term box) to use Google's SafeSearch program. This allows you to turn on their filter to prevent explicit text and images from appearing during a search.

- **When your child is surfing, require that he or she has a plan**, narrows the search, and watches spelling. (Some porn and hate sites use misspellings to ensure hits, for example "dinseyland"). Make sure your child knows how to leave a site, especially if he or she is "mouse-trapped" (the site keeps coming back when you are trying to leave it). The solution is to close down the Internet, and then log on again. You may also choose to disable Java to prevent pop-up windows that entice you with contests, great deals, or other "related" Web sites (which often lead to undesirable sites when they are selected).

- **Limit access to chat rooms, gaming sites, or popular social networking sites** such as Facebook and MySpace. Ideally, your child should only be in a chat room when you are in the room.

- **Learn which Web sites your child visits.** Surf the Net with him or her. Add the sites to your "Favorites" or "Bookmarks." Limit your child to visiting only the Web sites you have added to their favorites rather than random surfing. Monitor your child's Internet use by using the History button on your Internet browser's icon button.

- **Take time to "Google" your name and the names of members of your family** to see what information about you is on the Internet. Simply type in your name in the search box on the Google home page. You should also do a search on networking sites (such as

Facebook and MySpace) that you know your children have been visiting. If there is inappropriate information, you can have it removed and set up a privacy screen by going into Edit Profile or contacting the administrator (usually found at the bottom of the Web page under Contact Us).

- **Use firewalls and virus protection** to protect your computer from hackers, viruses, and other attacks from the sites you or your child may visit. Other software, such as Net Nanny, helps you monitor and regulate the sites your family may visit as well as set up filters that restrict the kind of information that your children can access. Update these programs regularly.

- **If your child is sending e-mail, set up a primary e-mail for close friends and family**; set up a shared e-mail account for you and your children or set up a dummy e-mail for your kids to give out to online friends or Web sites on which they must register to use. Consider using Yahoo or Hotmail for these accounts.

- **Make sure your child never gives out his or her real name**, passwords or any other information to chat room buddies, when registering at a site, or when taking part in a contest. Many Web sites that are attractive to young people, such as Neopets, Myscene, or sites for games and gaming, require registration before you can access the site. Decide on a dummy name and location to use when registering for new sites or contests. Make sure these names and passwords are added to your log.

- **Don't open a message from anyone you don't know.** Be on the lookout for friendly or exciting subject lines like "invitation," "you have won!" and "hi from an old friend."

- **Don't open any link on the Web site you are visiting**, even if it is flashing or pops up and tells you you've won a prize. Some even pretend your computer needs to be updated or has a problem. These links can easily take your children to sites that are not appropriate. Hit the Close button, or right-click and close the pop-up that way if you can't see a Close button.

- ◆ **Regularly go through your child's address book** and delete anyone your child can't identify as a friend.

- ◆ **Block bullying messages rather than replying.** You can access this tool through your Internet program (click on e-mail, then Options, then junk mail/spam filter).

- ◆ **Learn the language!** Text messaging is a new language (which is often intentional) and can look like Greek to those who aren't "in the loop"! See Appendix B for a guide to popular terms, such as LOL (laugh out loud) and CUL8R (see you later).

- ◆ **If you don't know much about the Internet, learn!** Many places, like public libraries and community colleges, may offer free courses on using the Net and e-mail. Or, even better, ask your child to teach you how to use the Internet—you'll not only learn how to use it, but you'll learn how your child uses it and what he or she values about it.

Since technology changes so rapidly, you need to familiarize yourself with what's happening out there in cyberspace. There are many excellent Web sites that give information helpful to parents such as www.symantec .com/norton/familyresources/index or http://www.netsmartz.org/ netparents.htm#. A sampling of these sites can be found in Appendix C, page 146.

Acronyms You Need to Know

POS = parent over shoulder	**ASL** = age, sex, location
PIR = parent in room	**LMIRL** = let's meet in real life
P911 = parent alert	**KPC** = keeping parents clueless
PAW = parents are watching	**ADR** or **ADDY** = address
PAL = parents are listening	**WYCM** = will you call me?

Securing an Active Defense in Cyberspace

As with schoolyard bullying, many children simply don't know what to do when they are being bullied online, so they don't do anything about it. Often, children don't report it because they are scared their computer will be taken away. Interestingly, some children who are bullied online then take out their anger and hurt by bullying others online.

A child may be being bullied online if he or she . . .

• Unexpectedly stops using the computer

• Appears nervous or jumpy when an instant message or e-mail appears

• Appears uneasy about going to school or outside in general

• Appears to be angry, depressed, or frustrated after using the computer

• Avoids discussions about what they are doing on the computer

• Becomes abnormally withdrawn from usual friends and family members

(Patchin & Hinduja, 2006)

It is essential for you and your child to realize that, once again, they have power in bullying situations. As with bullying "in the real world," bullies rely on secrecy and the acquiescence of their target. If a bullied child does not respond (even though it's a natural reaction, especially online, to defend yourself), the bully is denied the satisfaction of knowing their words have hit their target.

As you know, bullies don't like to be confronted with their actions or behaviors. When your child reports a bullying incident, especially to your Internet service provider (ISP), the bully can usually be tracked down and dealt with. If the bully makes threats or seems to know a lot of personal information, save and print all messages and then contact your local police department.

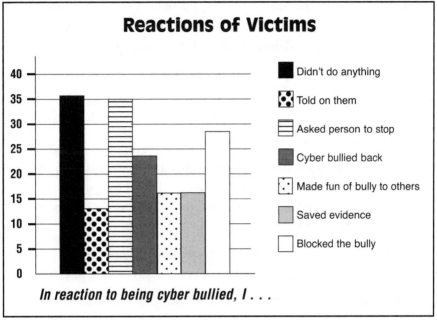

Reactions of Victims

In reaction to being cyber bullied, I . . .

From a workshop presented at the Annual Meeting of the International Bullying Prevention Association by Kowalski, R.M., Limber, S.P.,and Agatston, P.W. 2007.
http://www.cyberbullyhelp.com/images/effectofbullying-newresearch.pdf

Developing a Cyber-Bullying Plan

So the power you have is considerable. Have your child follow these important guidelines in creating his or her own cyber-bullying plan:

◆ Speak up and tell an adult if you are being bullied or feel uncomfortable at any Web site or chat room.

◆ Don't talk back to a bully, or argue or respond in any way, even if you feel you are being unfairly treated. If a bully gets no response, he or she may look elsewhere.

◆ If you are sent a bullying message, e-mail or text, save a copy of it and note the date and time. Advise your ISP of the problem by either phoning the provider's help line or forwarding the message with details to their customer service department. Your ISP should provide clear guidelines about their policies and procedures regarding cyber safety and cyber bullying on their Web site and respond quickly to problems.

♦ After you've made copies or saved the bullying messages, leave the site. Wait a couple of days, then return. If the bullying begins again, leave and don't go back. There are lots of other places to visit!

♦ Don't worry about offending others; if you are harassed or uncomfortable, get off the site.

♦ Many chat rooms have Report Abuse buttons. Use them to tell what's making you uncomfortable.

♦ If someone else is being bullied online, speak out about it. If you are tempted to join in, ask yourself, "Would I say this to someone face to face? How would I feel if someone said this to me?" Don't be a cyber-bully bystander.

♦ Have "safe code words" that you can use with good friends that help you make sure you know whom you are really talking to online.

Here's an example of one child's Cyber-Bullying Personal Plan:

Tanisha's Cyber-Bullying Personal Plan

If I am being bullied or I'm uncomfortable while I am on the Internet or e-mail, I will (not answer at all, even if the person is being really mean).

Then I will (go and get my parent right away. I won't turn off or erase the screen because we will make a copy of what the bully has said to me).

If that doesn't work, then I will (not visit that Web site again, or block the access of my e-mail to that sender; my parent will help me do this).

If I am bullied, I will tell (my parents, my older brother, and our Internet service provider).

All of these would be valuable additions to a cyber-bullying personal plan you could develop with your child. It might look something like the plan above. You can use the prompts in boldface as a starting point or rephrase the prompts to meet your child's specific needs. The words in parenthesis may resemble your child's responses.

In the box on page 139 is another example of a simple plan that could be posted by the family's computer.

Cyber-Bullying Personal Plan

If I get a bullying message, or a message that makes me uncomfortable, I will remember these steps. I will:

1. **Not respond** (even if what the person is saying is not true, unfair or it makes me angry)

2. **Save the message right away**

3. **Tell my parents**

4. **Together with a parent, block the sender** (in my e-mail program, I will click on Options and then go to the junk mail filter)

5. **Report the message to the Internet service provider**

What If My Child Is the Cyber Bully?

Being alert for signs of cyber bullying (see list on page 141) also means being alert to the possibility that your child may become involved in bullying behaviors. Much as we don't like to admit it, every child has opportunities to intimidate or harass someone else and to experience the often exciting feelings of power and control over others, and the Internet offers a relatively anonymous and easy way for children to experiment.

This is another reason why it's so important for you to have the computer out in the open and have your children clearly understand that you will be monitoring the things that they do online.

As discussed in Chapter Four, discovering whether bullying behaviors are becoming a pattern for your child is essential. Many, if not all of us, try to bully someone else at some point during our lives. The key experiences that stop bullying include an unsuccessful attempt to intimidate someone else, feelings of guilt or regret after the incident, and getting caught and being held accountable.

Discuss with your children your views on cyber bullying, why it is harmful, and what the consequences will be if he or she participates in cyber bullying. Your children must understand that bullying in the "virtual" world is just as serious as bullying in the real world, and make sure they realize that you will hold them accountable for any aggressive actions.

If your child is a cyber bully, there are three main actions you should take.

♦ **Hold your child accountable for the negative behavior** by having him or her write a letter of apology and an explanation of why he or she bullied the person and what he or she will do the next time. If you don't know the person your child was harassing (and this is likely), you should still have your child write the letter and then give it to you. If your child is traced and identified as a bully by your ISP provider, you will have a copy of the letter to send in response.

♦ **Make sure you have reasonable, firm consequences** for this kind of computer behavior. As discussed in Chapter Four, your child must have a clear understanding that if he or she bullies in any way, the consequences will be swift and meaningful.

♦ **Consider removing your child from the Internet** for a certain period of time. A first-time offense could result in withholding online access for two weeks, second offenses for a month, third offense, indefinitely. Your child can still use the computer for software games and word processing, but should not be able to access the Net.

Your child's teacher should also be informed of the bullying, especially if there are consequences that may affect his or her school work. If a child is not able to access the Internet from home, ask the teacher for some input. Should he or she still be able to use the Internet at school, with direct supervision? Could you or a school staff member come to the classroom and supervise your child if Internet access is necessary? Your child's teacher can be an important ally in dealing with the problem.

If your child has a pattern of cyber bullying, and does not respond to these interventions, then you may need further support to help him or her change this aggressive behavior. Chapter Four gives you ideas about whom to contact.

Cyber bullying may be a worrying trend, but there are things that you can do to protect your child. It may be appropriate to ask yourself which technologies you are comfortable with your child accessing. Does your child need a cell phone with a camera? Is a Web cam a necessary accessory for your family? Does your child need his or her own e-mail address?

Ultimately, the best prevention is education and awareness. By keeping tabs on your child's computer use, talking about cyber bullying, and staying up to date with the technology available, you will go a long way toward making cyber bullying in your household obsolete.

A child may be bullying others online if he or she . . .

• Quickly switches screens or closes programs as you walk by

• Uses the computer late at night

• Gets unusually upset if he or she cannot use the computer

• Laughs excessively while on the computer

• Avoids discussions about what he or she is doing on the computer

• Is using multiple online accounts, or an account that is not his or her own

(Adapted from Patchin & Hinduja, 2006)

Family Contract for Online Safety
(for Kids Under 8)

♦ I won't give out my address or telephone number, or the name and location of my school without my parents' permission. I will never send a person my picture or anything else without **first** checking with my parents.

♦ I won't give out my Internet passwords to **anyone** (even my best friend).

♦ **I will tell my parents right away if:**
  • I come across any information that makes me feel uncomfortable.
  • Someone I meet online wants me to send him or her a photo or meet me in person.
  • I get any messages that are mean or make me feel uncomfortable. It's not my fault if I get a message like that.
  • I want to download or install software or do anything that could possibly hurt our computer.
  • I get invitations to contests or am asked to respond to any unexpected messages when I am on the Internet. I won't respond until I have my parent's permission.

♦ If I am being bullied online, I will **not respond**; I will **save it**, and then tell my parents. We will **block the sender** and then **report it to our ISP.**

♦ I will be a good online citizen and not do anything that hurts other people or is against the law.

♦ My parents and I will set up rules for going online. We will decide upon the time of day that I can be online, the length of time I can be online, and appropriate areas for me to visit. I won't access other areas or break these rules without their permission, and I will keep a log of all of the Web sites I am registered at, and write down the username and password I have at each site.

♦ I will help my parents understand how to have fun and learn things online and teach them things about the Internet, computers and other technology.

♦ I agree to the above.

_____   _____
Child signs here   Date

♦ I will help my child follow this agreement and will allow reasonable use of the Internet as long as these rules and other family rules are followed.

_____   _____
Parent(s) or Guardian(s) sign here   Date

(Adapted from the brochure "Child Safety on the Information Highway"
by Lawrence J. Magid, and published by the National Center for
Missing and Exploited Children © 1997, 2005 Larry Magid)

Internet Use Contract

(for Kids 8 Through 12)

♦ As a family, we will set up rules for going online. We will decide upon the time of day that I can be online, the length of time I can be online, and appropriate areas for me to visit. I won't access other areas without my family's permission.

♦ I will never share personal information such as my address, my telephone number, my parent's or guardian's work address/telephone number, or the name and location of my school without permission.

♦ I won't give out my passwords to anyone.

♦ If asked to share photos, personal information, or anything that may identify me, I will ask permission before I send it. I will not download *anything* from *anyone* without permission. I will not enter contests or respond to any unexpected messages.

♦ I will keep a log of all of the Web sites where I am registered, and write the username and password for each one in the log.

♦ I will tell a trusted adult if I come across anything that makes me feel scared, uncomfortable, or confused.

♦ I will never respond to any messages that are mean or *in any way* make me feel uncomfortable. I will **not respond**, I will **save it**, and then I will tell my family. We will **block the sender** and then **report it to our ISP.**

♦ I will not send threatening or hurtful messages to anyone, for any reason. If I do, I understand the consequences for this behavior.

♦ I will never meet in person with anyone I have first "met" online without permission. If my family agrees to the meeting, it will be in a public place, and my family will come along.

♦ I agree to the above.

_____   _____

Child signs here   Date

As your parent/guardian, I will remain calm and open-minded when you tell me about any problems you are having on the Internet. I will support you in whatever way I can.

_____   _____

Parent(s) or Guardian(s) sign here   Date

(*Adapted from www.getwebwise.ca/parent_family_contracts.cfm*)

Parents' Pledge

♦ I will get to know the services and Web sites my child uses. If I don't know how to use them, I'll get my child or a knowledgeable adult to show me.

♦ My family and I will set reasonable rules and guidelines for computer use and will discuss these rules and post them near the computer as a reminder.

♦ I will also abide by the rules of use our family decides upon.

♦ I'll remember to regularly monitor my child's compliance with these rules, and will check up on the sites my child has visited.

♦ I will not overreact if my child tells me about a problem he or she is having on the Internet. Instead, we'll work together to try to solve the problem and prevent it from happening again.

♦ If our computer is used to threaten or harass others for any reason, the consequences will be swift and severe. We have discussed these consequences so we are all aware of what would happen if cyber bullying occurred.

♦ I will try to get to know my child's "online friends" just as I try to get to know his or her other friends.

_____   _____
Parent(s) or Guardian(s) sign here   Date

♦ I understand that my parent(s) agree to these rules and agree to help explore the Internet with me.

_____   _____
Child signs here   Date

(Adapted from the brochure "Child Safety on the Information Highway" by Lawrence J. Magid, and published by the National Center for Missing and Exploited Children © 1997, 2005 Larry Magid)

APPENDIX B

Chat Room Lingo

Even the most computer-literate parent may need help in understanding a child's Internet world—especially in the ultra-insider arena of chat rooms. The following are acronyms for common phrases used in chat rooms, gathered by Symantec, an Internet security company.

Are Your Kids Safe on the Internet?
AFAIK = as far as I know!

AFK = away from keyboard

ASL = age, sex, location

BB = bathroom break

BBL = be back later

BBS = be back soon

BF = boyfriend

BRB = be right back

BTW = by the way

CUL8R or
CULR = see you later

CUZ = because

DN = don't know

FYI = for your information

G2G or
GG = got to go

GF = girlfriend

HW = homework

IDC = I don't care

IDK = I don't know

IMO = in my opinion

JAS = just a second

JK = just kidding

KOTC = kiss on the cheek

LOL = laugh out loud

LYL = love you lots

LYLAS or
LYLAB = love you like a sister or love you like a brother

NM or
NVM = never mind

NP = no problem

OMG = Oh, my God

OTOH = on the other hand

POS = parent over shoulder

ROFLOL = rolling on floor laughing out loud

SN = screen name

SRY = sorry

SUP = What's up

SW = so what?

TMI = too much information

TTYL = talk to you later

TY = thank you

U = you

Y = why

(Adapted from www.topics-az.parenthood.com/articles.html?article_id=4787)

APPENDIX C

A List of Online Resources

There are many resources online designed to help you find your way through the Internet world. Many of the sites listed below give overviews and specifics on many aspects of computer use, and all of them provide good information about protecting your children online.

CTAP Region IV
California Technology Assistance Project
This site, funded by the state of California for its public school students, provides education materials and workshop downloads on a variety of topics, including cyber bullying.
http://www.ctap4.org/cybersafety/

ConnectSafely
A Project of the Tech Parenting Group
This site for Net safety education offers a forum for parents, teens, and experts to discuss safe socializing on the Web.
http://www.connectsafely.org/
ConnectSafely is a sister site to SafeKids.com, SafeTeens.com, and NetFamilyNews.org.

Cyberbully411
Internet Solutions for Kids, Inc.
Ideal for tweens and teenagers, this site offers resources to children interested in learning more about preventing cyber bullying and Internet harassment. Provides advice about tackling depression, communicating with parents, and more.
http://www.cyberbully411.org/

GetNetWise
Internet Education Foundation
Includes links for learning about safe searching, social networking, and reporting trouble. Plus, quick links to safe family-appropriate Web sites.
http://kids.getnetwise.org/

NetSmartz Workshop
National Center for Missing & Exploited Children
This must-see site offers both online and offline learning activities for parents and their children. Features include links to videos from experts and downloadable guides and presentations.
http://www.netsmartz.org/

A Parent's Guide for Children Ages 8 & 9: Safety and the Internet
The Canadian Centre for Child Protection
Here's a brochure to help parents of children in this age group. Includes steps parents and children can take to surf safely.
http://www.attorneygeneral.jus.gov.on.ca/english/news/2008/20080213-cfm_safety_8_9_en_ont.pdf

A Parent's Guide to Internet Safety
Federal Bureau of Investigation: Cyber Division
This site is designed to help parents learn about and support their children's online explorations and offers a downloadable pamphlet.
http://www.fbi.gov/publications/pguide/pguidee.htm

A Parent's Guide to the Online World
Royal Canadian Mounted Police: Deal.org
This resource can help parents navigate some of the risks and dangers associated with the Internet.
http://www.deal.org/content/index.php?option=com_content&task=view&id=574&Itemid=643

Parent Resource Center
IKeepSafe Coalition
Information about online safety provides quick links to the IKeepSafe Video Series, including videos on cyber bullying.
http://www.ikeepsafe.org/PRC/

ParentsCentre: Using Computers and the Internet
Department for Children, Schools and Families, UK
Here's a site you'll want to visit when you're talking with your children

about using the Internet. Look for the link titled Family Code, which provides pointers for setting rules and expectations.
http://www.parentscentre.gov.uk/usingcomputersandtheinternet/

Toolbox
StaySafe
Learn how to protect yourself and your family by keeping current with technology. Offers safety information on Chat Rooms, social networking, games, and more.
http://www.staysafe.org//toolbox/default.html

Wiredsafety: Information for Parents
Wired Kids, Inc.
Visit this site, the largest of its kind, to find information about online risks and to download Parenting Online, a guide for parents that is available in both English and Spanish.
http://www.wiredsafety.org/parent.html

Web Site Log

Child's Name & Date Registered	Parent O.K.	Complete Web Site Address	Username, Password	Type of Web Site (for example, gaming, chat room, e-mail, Web page)
Riley 6/15/08	Mom	www.kidsgamz.com	billyj Pword: Fido644	games

REFERENCES

Professional Resources Cited

Babcock, G. (January 24, 2007). *Survey finds children misunderstand public nature of the Internet.* Internet safety study conducted by Microsoft Canada and Ipsos Reid Survey. Toronto, Canada: Ispos News Center.

Banks, R. (1997). *Bullying in schools.* http://www.ed.gov/databases/ERIC_Digests/ed407154.html. (1999, November.) ERIC Digest No. ED407154.

Beran, T. N. & Violato, C. (2004). A model of childhood perceived peer harassment: Analyses of the Canadian national longitudinal survey of children and youth data. Washington, DC: *The Journal of Psychology, 138*(2), 129–148.

Brodkin, A. M. (2001). *Fresh approaches to working with problematic behavior.* New York: Scholastic.

Byrne, R. (2006). *The 2,548 best things anybody ever said.* New York: Simon & Schuster.

Caldwell, A. (April 20, 2004). Columbine: A recurring nightmare. Denver, CO: *Denver Post.*

Cox Communications with the National Centre for Missing and Exploited Children. (February 2005). *Parents Internet monitoring study.* Atlanta, Georgia.

Coloroso, B. (2003). *The bully, the bullied, and the bystander.* New York: Harper.

Coloroso, B. (2002). *Kids are worth it: Giving your child the gift of inner discipline.* New York: Quill.

Delville, Y., Melloni, Jr., R. H., & Ferris, C. F. (1998). Behavioral and neuro-biological consequences of social subjugation during puberty in golden hamsters. Washington, DC: *The Journal of Neuroscience*, April, *18*(7): 2667–2672.

Elman, N. M., & Kennedy-Moore, E. (2003). *The unwritten rules of friendship: Simple strategies to help your child make friends.* New York: Little, Brown and Company.

Environics Research Group (2001). *Young Canadians in a wired world.* Ottawa, Canada: Media Awareness Network and the Government of Canada.

Garrity, C. (2004). *Bully-proofing your school.* Longmont, CO: Sopris West.

Goleman, D. (1995). *Emotional intelligence: Why it can matter more than I.Q.* New York: Bantam Books.

Greenspan, S. (1995). *The challenging child.* Reading, MA: Addison Wesley.

Ha, T. T. (April 7, 2006). Star Wars kid cuts a deal with his tormentors. Toronto, Canada: *Globe and Mail.*

His Holiness the Dalai Lama (2006). *How to see yourself as you really are.* New York: Atria Books.

Kowalski, R. M., Limber, S. P., & Agatston, P. W. (2007). *Cyber bullying.* Workshop presented at the Annual Meeting of the International Bullying Prevention Association. Fort Lauderdale, FL. www.cyberbullyhelp.com.

Kutner, L. (October 2007). *How children develop empathy.* www.drkutner.com.

Macdonald, K. (November 30, 2006). Calgary, Canada: Calgary Police Service's Crime Prevention Unit.

Magid, L. J. (1997, 2005). *Child safety on the information highway.* Alexandria, Virginia: National Center for Missing & Exploited Children.

Marano, H. E. (1998). *Why doesn't anybody like me?* New York: William Morrow.

Markway, B. & Markway, G. (2005). *Nurturing the shy child.* New York: Thomas Dunne Books.

Marr, N. & Field, T. (2001). *Bullycide.* United Kingdom: Success Unlimited Publishing.

McMullen, C. (2005). *Creating a bully-free classroom.* New York: Scholastic.

Nansel, T. R., Overpeck, M., Pilla, R. S., Ran, J., Simons-Morton, B. & Scheidt, P. (2001). Bullying behaviors among U.S. youth: Prevalence and association with psychosocial adjustment. Chicago: *Journal of the American Medical Association, 285*, 2094–2100.

Nauert, R. (July 2008). *Brain scans demonstrate a child's empathy.* http://psychcentral.com.

National Criminal Justice References Service (2000). *Preventing school shootings.* Safe School Initiative Report, U.S. Secret Service. www.ncjrs.org/pdffiles1.

Noll, K. (2008). *Taking the bully by the horns: Books and workshops on bullying, school violence, and self-esteem issues.* http://kathynoll.wordpress.com/bully-blog/.

Olweus, D. (1993). *Bullying at school.* Cambridge, MA: Blackwell.

Patchin, J. W. & Hinduja, S. (2006). Bullies move beyond the schoolyard: A preliminary look at cyberbullying. Thousand Oaks, CA: *Youth Violence and Juvenile Justice, 4*(2), 148–169.

Sheras, P. (2002). *Your child: Bully or victim?: Understanding and ending schoolyard tyranny.* New York: Simon and Schuster.

Szpir, M. (1998). Angry adolescent brains. Research Triangle Park, NC: *American Scientist, The Magazine of Sigma Xi, 86*(4).

Teolis, B. (1998). *Ready-to-use conflict resolution activities.* New York: Scholastic.

Thompson, A. M. (1996). Attention deficit hyperactivity disorder: A parent's perspective. Bloomington, IN: *Phi Delta Kappan*, 434.

Wilson, S. (2005). *Safe kids, safe families.* New York: HarperCollins.

Wolke, D., Woods, S., Bloomfield, L., Karstadt, L. (2001). Bullying involvement in primary school and common health problems. Hatfield, United Kingdom: *Archives of Disease in Childhood, 85*:197–201, September.

Children's Literature Cited

Boyd, L. (1989). *Bailey the big bully.* New York: Viking Kestrel.

Caseley, J. (2001). *Bully.* New York: Greenwillow Books.

Cosby, B. (1997). *The meanest thing to say.* New York: Scholastic.

Cox, J. (1999). *Mean, mean Maureen Green.* New York: Holiday House.

Crary, E. (1982). *I want it.* Seattle, WA: Parenting Press.

Griff, P. R. (1988). *B-E-S-T friends.* New York: Bantam Doubleday.

Hoff, S. (1985). *Who will be my friends?* New York: HarperCollins.

Leedy, L. (1996). *How humans make friends.* New York: Holiday House.

Levete, S. (1998). *How do I feel about . . . making friends.* Brookfield, CT: Copper Beech Books.

Lovell, P. (2001). *Stand tall, Mary Lou Melon.* New York: G. P. Putnam's Sons.

Ludwig, T. (2004). *My secret bully.* Berkeley: Tricycle Press.

McCain, B. (2001). *Nobody knew what to do.* Morton Grove, Illinois: Albert Whitman and Co.

Michelle, L. (1995). *How kids make friends . . . secrets for making lots of friends, no matter how shy you are.* Buffalo Grove, Illinois: Freedom Press.

Piper, W. (1978). *The little engine that could.* New York: Grosset and Dunlap.

Romain, T. (1997). *Bullies are a pain in the brain.* Minneapolis: Free Spirit Publishing.

Index